CAMBRIDGE LIBRARY COLLECTION

Books of enduring scholarly value

Women's Writing

The later twentieth century saw a huge wave of academic interest in women's writing, which led to the rediscovery of neglected works from a wide range of genres, periods and languages. Many books that were immensely popular and influential in their own day are now studied again, both for their own sake and for what they reveal about the social, political and cultural conditions of their time. A pioneering resource in this area is Orlando: Women's Writing in the British Isles from the Beginnings to the Present (http://orlando.cambridge.org), which provides entries on authors' lives and writing careers, contextual material, timelines, sets of internal links, and bibliographies. Its editors have made a major contribution to the selection of the works reissued in this series within the Cambridge Library Collection, which focuses on non-fiction publications by women on a wide range of subjects from astronomy to biography, music to political economy, and education to prison reform.

Essays on Woman's Work

Bessie Rayner Parkes (1829–1925) was an English poet, writer and prominent early feminist best known for her campaigns for women's right to work and receive professional training. With Barbara Bodichon (1827–91), she founded the first English feminist journal, *The English Woman's Review* in 1858. Parkes served as its principal editor between 1858 and 1864. This volume, first published in 1865 and containing several essays from *The English Woman's Review* advocates for young middle-class women to be given the opportunity to work and earn a living in safe conditions with fair pay. Parkes links the changes in society caused by the Industrial Revolution to the need for women to work. Her reassurance that married women should still be supported by their husbands illustrates how Parkes, like many other feminists, worked within the contemporary social framework and used existing social norms to justify her aims. For more information on this author, see http://orlando.cambridge.org/public/svPeople?person_id=parkbe

T0370805

Cambridge University Press has long been a pioneer in the reissuing of out-of-print titles from its own backlist, producing digital reprints of books that are still sought after by scholars and students but could not be reprinted economically using traditional technology. The Cambridge Library Collection extends this activity to a wider range of books which are still of importance to researchers and professionals, either for the source material they contain, or as landmarks in the history of their academic discipline.

Drawing from the world-renowned collections in the Cambridge University Library, and guided by the advice of experts in each subject area, Cambridge University Press is using state-of-the-art scanning machines in its own Printing House to capture the content of each book selected for inclusion. The files are processed to give a consistently clear, crisp image, and the books finished to the high quality standard for which the Press is recognised around the world. The latest print-on-demand technology ensures that the books will remain available indefinitely, and that orders for single or multiple copies can quickly be supplied.

The Cambridge Library Collection will bring back to life books of enduring scholarly value (including out-of-copyright works originally issued by other publishers) across a wide range of disciplines in the humanities and social sciences and in science and technology.

Essays on Woman's Work

BESSIE RAYNER PARKES

CAMBRIDGE UNIVERSITY PRESS

Cambridge, New York, Melbourne, Madrid, Cape Town, Singapore,
São Paolo, Delhi, Dubai, Tokyo, Mexico City

Published in the United States of America by Cambridge University Press, New York

www.cambridge.org
Information on this title: www.cambridge.org/9781108020817

© in this compilation Cambridge University Press 2010

This edition first published 1865
This digitally printed version 2010

ISBN 978-1-108-02081-7 Paperback

This book reproduces the text of the original edition. The content and language reflect
the beliefs, practices and terminology of their time, and have not been updated.

Cambridge University Press wishes to make clear that the book, unless originally published
by Cambridge, is not being republished by, in association or collaboration with, or
with the endorsement or approval of, the original publisher or its successors in title.

ESSAYS ON WOMAN'S WORK.

ESSAYS ON WOMAN'S WORK

BY

BESSIE RAYNER PARKES

Anchora Spei

ALEXANDER STRAHAN, PUBLISHER
148 STRAND, LONDON
1865

THESE ESSAYS,

COMPOSED DURING EIGHT YEARS PASSED WITH

MANY FELLOW-WORKERS

IN INVESTIGATING THE CONDITION

OF THE EDUCATED WORKING WOMEN OF ENGLAND,

Are Dedicated

TO THE DEAR AND HONOURED MEMORY OF

ANNA JAMESON.

CONTENTS.

I.

INTRODUCTORY.

INTRODUCTORY.

IN gathering together the data afforded by the movement of the last ten years, it will be well to prefix a chapter on the reasons which have dictated the effort to improve the condition of women in our time and country. These reasons, drawn out in detail, would probably prove to be as various as the mind and characters of those engaged in the work. Questions which involve the education, employment, morals, and manners of one sex, are, of course, subordinate to those deeper philosophical and religious questions which concern the whole of humanity; and they will be judged according to the general intellectual cast, and, in great measure, according to the religious belief, of each individual. The very first point which every human being has to settle, and which every one does settle in some sort of

rough way, is, what is admirable and desirable,—
what is the *beau-ideal* for the human creature ? The
catechism supplies a very definite answer in regard
to the end for which we were created. Nevertheless
it is not one in our time universally accepted ; and
a great many other theories have either superseded,
or so far mixed themselves up with that old-
fashioned answer, as materially to change its practical effect.

Goethe, for instance, considered that self-cul-
ture and full development of the body and brain,
with the decent and moderate enjoyment of all
faculties of the same, constituted the *beau-ideal;* and
Margaret Fuller Ossoli was largely influenced by
his general theory of life, when she wrote of " Women in the Nineteenth Century," though her affec-
tionate nature redeemed its refined selfishness.
Fifty years earlier the world was full of political
theories, and of the semi-scientific, semi-moral
ideas which showed their best in Miss Edgeworth's
books. It followed as a matter of course that
Mary Wollstonecraft's volume on the " Rights of
Woman " was coloured by the solemn, sententious,
and intensely reasoning element which prevailed

in her generation. At the very same time, however, the master mind of John Wesley had planted
in English society the seeds of evangelical reform;
and another theory of female excellence, nobly
illustrated by Mrs Fletcher of Madeley and Hannah More, began to appear in literature. Again,
in the early part of our own generation, the great
legal agitations of the Reform Bill, and of the
Repeal of the Corn-Laws, excited the public mind
in the direction of legal improvements; and those
who were interested in the welfare of women began
to turn their attention to the innumerable cases in
which they suffered from the law of property as
affected by marriage. Lastly, during the whole of
this century a strong humanitarian element has
prevailed, compassionating poverty, hunger and
cold; and women having shared the benefit, the
late industrial movement has been the result.

Here, then, we have five different ideas, each of
which has been prolific in results; five different
theories which said—

Let women be thoroughly developed.

Let women be thoroughly rational.

Let women be pious and charitable.

Let women be properly protected by law.

Let women have fair chances of a livelihood.

And lastly, a sixth demand is now being actively pressed, namely, let women have ample access to all stores of learning,—a demand for education, which, though it has something of the same sound, is, in reality, different from Goethe's culture or Mary Wollstonecraft's rationality; for the male thinker required a large admixture of the artistic and emotional experiences, and the authoress laid much greater stress upon a kind of broad common sense and right reason than upon acquired knowledge,—while the desire of imparting an ample measure of education, and of being permitted to test the result by authoritative examinations, is part of the general effect of the schoolmaster being abroad.

As in the theoretic, so in the practical part of every social movement, the measures taken in regard to any given subject will be found to vary with the deeper belief of those who act. In politics, the reliance on universal suffrage accompanies a highly favourable view of the sense and virtue of average human nature, and the reliance on des-

potism, a hopelessly low view of the same ; in
education, a broadcast method of instruction implies a fond belief that the child has every chance
of distinguishing good from evil, and a very narrow
training denies any such expectation ; and in the
bringing up of girls, a very unrestricted liberty
argues a belief in the mind of the guardian that the
chances are eminently in favour of their going right,
and an incessant watchfulness implies just the reverse. Again, the different methods of training
both boys and girls are, in reality, divided by a different aim as to the kind of man and woman to
be achieved. Are we to care most about the body
and brain, all that comes under the head of natural
organisation, or are we to be particularly anxious
aboùt that mysterious part of us which all Christians
recognise as being different from either—the soul?
Are we to think most of virtue and innocence, or are
we to take every pains towards securing liberty and
opportunities of action? Are we to trouble ourselves chiefly about the duties which boys and girls
will in future have to fulfil, or about the advantages
they have a right to enjoy? Does it very much
matter if, in securing these advantages to the

greater number, a certain percentage suffer grievous loss? Many people of excellent intention are found in this generation to hold extremely opposite views on such questions as these; and therefore it is no wonder that, on the subordinate questions affecting women alone, their judgments should also differ; and we must not be surprised to find that a marked diversity of practical aims has existed among the supporters of what has been generally known as the woman's movement, or that it should be quite impossible to draw up any definite programme of what they wanted or strove to attain. There is, however, one point upon which every one has combined, and that is, the industrial movement; for here the need was glaring, and the remedy simple, though difficult of attainment,—more work, and more wages to purchase more food and more clothing; that everybody can understand, and nobody can well differ about.

My own opinion upon the general question of the position, treatment, and value of women in modern society may be briefly stated; and I am aware that it differs almost equally from what may be called the radical and the conservative points of view. I believe that now, as in all ages of the world, the substantial equality of nature renders the two sexes of equal weight and value in the moral world, and that their action upon each other in every relation of life is far too complex to admit of any great difference between them in any given rank. I do not believe in the accuracy of the observations of any woman who says that English women are at this moment inferior to English men in general sense and intelligence, and ought *not* to remain so; any more than I believe in the accuracy of the observation of any man who comes to a similar opinion, with this difference, that he thinks they *ought* so to remain. I believe that, in both cases, the false judgment arises from an enormous overrating of the value of acquired education, as compared to general intellectual and moral power. I have never seen families, in any rank, where the brothers were good and clever, and the sisters frivolous fools. There are bad men and bad women, foolish men and foolish women, ignorant men and ignorant women; but I believe the average of the two halves of humanity to be at any given time much the same. Men get more school

knowledge, and, of course, they get more professional training; and if I wanted a technical judgment of any kind, of course I should apply to a
man, but if I wanted a good honest judgment on a
question of conduct, I should go to a good man or
woman indifferently; and if it were a matter re-
quiring wholesome knowledge of the world, I would
as soon go to an old woman as to an old man, and
should expect to get as sensible an opinion. It
appears to me that men and women are both apt
to be warped in their minds, but from opposite
causes; and I do not think the chances of a false
bias greater in the one than in the other. Taken
together, they make up the mass of sinning, suffering, striving humanity; and if I wish to work especially for women, it is because I am a woman
myself, and so able to appreciate their particular
troubles.

It is very good for all who habitually dwell in
the atmosphere of any social question to go for
awhile into scenes where its large proportions
assume the likeness of a dream, standing, it may
be, in mountainous reality upon the horizon, yet
so softened by distance, and rendered delicate by

intervening air, that its size and importance, its difficult heights and dangerous chasms, are lost in the fair, faint lines of its form, as it rises afar off in the pale depths of the sky. Some years ago I left London, where for many months I had been intensely engaged in work pertaining to the *English Woman's Journal*, and spent a couple of months in Rome. It was then that, having ascended, as travellers are wont to do, to the top of the enormous arches of the Baths of Caracalla, and seeing on either hand the distant mountain-ranges which encircle the Eternal City, this simile came home to me with a living and peculiar force. There was a world beyond the mountains, a world of activities and reforms; but its murmur was there unheard. There is a life of the conscience, as distinguished from the purely spiritual life; and here it seemed as if the practical mundane conscience had retreated into the background, and the soul had it all her own way. I never had felt in Italy the want of those particular ideas of social and moral activity which form the daily portion of every English or American man, woman, and child, any more than I now believe in the

permanent engrafting of them upon the Italian
race.   Their own perfection they can doubtless
attain, but it is not that of the northern peoples.
Considered, therefore, from that southern land,
thoughts which seem at home to possess round-
ness and completeness, sink into mere parts of
the whole; and aims which are all-absorbing in
London, are reduced in proportion when measured
against the vastness of Rome, whose history em-
braces many ages of time, and three great empires
of faith, and as many mighty dominions in politics,
social and domestic.   It may easily be imagined
that, sitting high up amidst the gigantic ruins, and
looking out over the domes and towers on to the
broad gray sweeps of the Campagna, from Albano
to Soracte, my mind should revert to the home
work, to the ferment of thought and feeling in our
periodical press, and particularly to the numerous
discussions everywhere rising upon the claims and
the duties of women, to the stirring life which
rested not an hour, while that calm setting sun,
sinking into the western waters of the Mediter-
ranean, touched with crimson the pinnacles of St
John Lateran and the round roof of St Ste-

fano on the Cælian Hill, and lit up the green slopes where Tusculun and Alba Longa are seen no more.

As I looked over this immense expanse, there suddenly rose before my mind a vision of the countless multitude of women who have here lived and died. Women of many nations, and of many faiths: Etruscans, adorned with fine gold, very proud in their ancient lineage, allied both to Egypt and to Greece; Romans of the regal, the republican, and the imperial times, women who lived under the most despotic and the most just laws, and who were virtuous and respected under the first epoch, and debased and degraded at the very time when they had secured so much of freedom. Then I thought of the early Christian women, saints, virgins, and martyrs; of the armies of nuns whose rule had gone forth from Rome, and of hundreds still busy within its walls, praying, teaching, or tending the sick; of women who were brave in the old times, and feared neither the axe, nor the stake, nor the hungry war of beasts in that very Colosseum which lifted its ruined arches before me in the red radiance. One half of the great

nations of antiquity, one half of the church mili-
tant,—these were women, and as I looked abroad
over Rome, and thought of them, I felt how par-
tial are the efforts of any particular nation in the
solving of moral questions which have found, from
age to age, some sort of practical solution in a
million homes.

Let none think this reflection far-fetched. It is
impossible to travel, by the power of steam, with
sudden swiftness from one country to another, from
the metropolis of the present to the metropolis of
the past, from England to Italy, from London to
Rome, without being powerfully impressed by the
moral contrast, which receives no softening, as in
the old days of posting, from many new images
received on the road. The steamer and the rail-
road afford but little food for fresh thought, and
the transition seems sudden and complete. And
when, up to the last hour of English life, the mind
had been perforce absorbed in the working out of
one idea, how wonderful, how impressive it was to
find oneself where that idea had no practical moment, where it seemed to hinge upon nothing past,
present, or future, or to be clothed in forms with

which we find it hard to sympathise, and to await no future developments other than those it has attained in the past.

Yet the life which God appointed has been in full play here for many thousand years. There is no spot on earth where rival faiths have so freely contended, where the great drama of existence may be considered to have been so fairly played out. Surely one who honestly desires to learn truth in social morals may find both the principles and their examples in some age of Rome.

Now I will freely confess that one thought was uppermost in my mind whenever I walked among these ruins, and inly contrasted that which I had left and that which I found: our schools and mechanics' institutes and periodicals, with this population of black-haired, black-eyed gossips, who seem to study nothing under heaven, and the general condition of Italian women, who never give token of distinctive life. It is in brief this,—that these millions of women must have realised, in the aggregate, the destiny which they were intended to fulfil, or the wheels of the antique world would have stopped working.

The mass of men are intended to wrestle with the earth and its products for subsistence; the mass of women are intended to apply the fruits of that toil. In this common and inglorious career Heaven has ordained that the finer elements of heart and soul shall grow like flowers from the soil. The most ordinary duties and affections are the most precious; and, whether exercised by men or by women, in the busy north or in the tranquil south, they form the truest ground for mutual con fidence and respect.

While, therefore, deprecating any participation in the opinion which regards women as lamentably inferior to men in the elements of mind and character, which form the true worth of a human being, I would assist heartily any endeavour to help them onwards towards the standard of excellence and efficiency which all should strive to attain. And I do consider it to be the especial business of a woman to work for her own sex, because she may reasonably be supposed to best know its needs and capabilities; and I feel the greatest sympathy with all practical efforts, provided the arguments upon which they are based be not strained too far, so as to become narrow and *doctrindire*.

There is, however, one great and serious exception, one sad discrepancy between the lot of the two sexes in our time, one upon which no person of observation can honestly refuse to be convinced, and the recognition of which commits to no theory of any kind. This discrepancy is of modern origin, and I fear the mischief it causes is still increasing in spite of recent efforts to stem the tide; for all the purely economical action of modern civilisation seems tending to its increase, and the counteractives have not yet been generally sought or applied, though they have been much talked about. I allude to the difficulty experienced by large classes of women in making a bare livelihood, which nevertheless they are expected to provide for themselves.

Among the changes incident to the mechanical progress of the last hundred years, is one of which little historical note has been taken, but which has made a mighty revolution in the domestic manners of an immense body of our population. The

B

subdivision of labour has withdrawn manufactures from under the household roof, and gathered them into huge centres of industry, whence the products are again distributed far and wide—the enormous increase of our population, the facilities of transit, the perfecting of our commercial system,—all these influences have created a totally new kind of life for the lower classes, and included in the transformation is the vast change which the century has brought about in the condition, in the very ideal of life, of the working women of England and France. I couple the two countries together because they essentially represent all that is implied in modern civilisation, its benefits and its evils, in an almost equal degree; for if England has in some respects an advantage in the race, be sure that France is pursuing with giant strides, and that her capitalists and her workpeople are fast becoming the duplicates of our own.

Every one agrees, to judge by the incessant reference to it in the newspapers, that there is a certain phase of European life, peculiar to our generation and that of our fathers, which is so distinctly marked that it is indeed modern civilisation.

Some years ago, when Charles Mackay's songs were popular in the streets, it was generally said to be the dawn of something quite new and splendid in the earth's history, the immediate herald of "the good time coming;" but a strong reaction has taken place towards an appreciation of mediæval times; Mr Ruskin, Mr Froude, and a host of lesser men, have done battle for the dark ages, and it is now generally conceded that Venice, Florence, and Holland possessed in their palmy days a very respectable civilisation of their own.

Whether, however, it be a marked growth, or only a marked change, it is evident that our ways are not as their ways, and that an immense increase of products, and a striking uniformity in what we produce, together with a constantly extending diffusion of material and intellectual goods, are the characteristics of the age of steam. England and France exhibit them in every department of their public and private life, and the treaty of commerce was destined to increase them greatly, by stimulating each country to production of its own specialities, so that all France, unless it goes to bed by gaslight, will probably adopt Birmingham candlesticks, and our Queen's subjects will more than ever be ruled in their costume by the fiats of Lyons and Paris for the year.

And how unheeded is the *price* at which this great European change has been accomplished : the price which has been silently levied in every manufacturing town in both kingdoms—the great revolution which has been so little noticed amidst the noise of politics and the clash of war—the withdrawal of women from the life of the household, and the suction of them by hundreds of thousands within the vortex of industrial life.

It is not at first easy to grasp the vast reality of the change. Figures alone do not always impress the imagination ; so many women in the cotton trade, so many in the woollen ; but the mind loses its track among the *oughts,* just as the savage gets bewildered beyond his own ten digits. But in considering the case of governesses, and why there seems to be such an inexplicable amount of suffering in that class, we are brought face to face with these wider and deeper questions, and see that their actual destitution, though specially the result of overflowing numbers, is but part of a general tendency on the part of modern civilisation to cast on women the responsibility of being their own breadwinners, and to say to them with a thousand tongues, "If ye will not work, neither shall ye eat."

Look at the present constitution of Lancashire life. When the American war hindered the supply of cotton to such an extent that, before we could reckon on supplies from our Indian empire or elsewhere, the mill hands were thrown out of employ, *who* were the sufferers? Who were at least a majority of the total of the workpeople? Women and girls. My readers know what it is in Lancashire: those miles upon miles of dusky red dwellings, those acres of huge factories, those endless rows of spinning and weaving machines, each with its patient industrious female "hand." If a catastrophe falls on Yorkshire, and the chimneys of Bradford or Halifax cease to smoke, who are they that come upon the poor-rates or hunger at home? Women and girls. I was told in Manchester, by one of the most eminent and thoughtful women in England, that the outpouring of a mill in full work at the hour of dinner was such a torrent of living humanity that a lady could not walk against the stream: I was told the same thing at Bradford, by a female friend. In both instances the quitting of the mill seemed to have struck their imaginations as a typical moment, and they spoke of it as something which once seen could not be forgotten.

At Nottingham and Leicester, which I visited in 1861, the women are so absorbed into the mills and warehouses that little is known of female destitution. In Birmingham, where vast numbers of women are employed in the lighter branches of the metal trade, they may be seen working in the button manufacture, in japanning, in pin and needle making. In Staffordshire they make nails ; and unless my readers have seen them, I cannot represent to the imagination the extraordinary figures they present—black with soot, muscular, brawny—undelightful to the last degree. In mines they are no longer allowed to work ; but remember that they did work there not so long ago, taking with men an equal chance of fire-damp and drowning, even sometimes being harnessed to the carts if poor patient horses were too dear.

I read once of a whipmakers' strike, which took place because women were being introduced into a branch of work for which men had hitherto been employed; but perhaps the most impressive thing which ever came to my immediate knowledge was the description in a small country paper of a factory strike, in which a prolonged irritation existed between the hands and the very excellent firm owning the works. There were letters and speeches to and fro; placards on the walls, and a liberal expenditure of forcible Saxon language. Now, who were these hands "out on strike?" these people who made speeches, gathered together in angry knots at the corners of the streets? —Women!

After this, may I not say, that on no small body of ladies in London, on no committees or societies trying to struggle with the wants of the time, can rest the charge of unsexing women by advising them to follow new paths, away from household shelter and natural duties, when a mighty and all-pervading power, the power of trade, renders the workman's home empty of the house-mother's presence for ten hours a day, and teaches English women the advantage of being "out on strike?"

For it is clear that, since modern society will have it so, women must work: "weeping," which Mr Kingsley regards as their appropriate employment, in fishing villages and elsewhere, being no longer to the purpose. I do not say that these myriads are, on the whole, ill-paid, ill-fed, sickly, or immoral; I only wish to point to the fact that they are actually working, and, for the most part, in non-domestic labour, a labour which cannot be carried on under a husbands or a father's roof. And recognising this apparently hopeless necessity, I believe it to be just and advisable that printing and all such trades be fairly thrown open to them; for we have to do with hunger and thirst and cold; with an imperious need of meat and drink, and fire and clothing; and, moreover, as trade uses women up so freely whenever it finds them cheaper than men, they themselves have a just claim to the good along with the evil, and, being forced into industrial life, it is for them to choose, if possible, any work for which their tenderer, feebler physical powers seem particularly adapted.

Let us now turn to France. It is some years since I was in Lyons, and with the introductions of M. Arles Dufour, one of the leading merchants and most enlightened economists of France, visited several of the *ateliers* where not more than six women are employed in the silk-weaving, under a mistress, or where sometimes the family only work among themselves. The conditions of this manufacture are very peculiar, the silk being bought by the merchants and allotted to the weavers, who bring it to the warehouse in a finished state, so that there is a singular absence of the bustle of English trade; there is comparatively little speculation, and in many ways the work is conducted in a mode rendering it easy for the female workers.

Little by little there may be seen, however, a tendency to an industrial change. This subject is amply and eloquently discussed in those remarkable articles, from the pen of M. Jules Simon, which appeared in the *Revue des Deux Mondes*, and which were gathered into a volume entitled "*L' Ouvrière.*" He believes that the greater production which steam power creates will gradu-

ally tempt the Lyonese merchants to turn into
master manufacturers, destroying the *ateliers* and
the family work in common.   At the time of my
visit I only heard of one establishment actually
in work on a large scale, and that was some miles
out of the town, and had been created chiefly on a
religious and charitable basis, that is to say, the
young female apprentices were bound for three
years, and were under charge of a community of
religious women ; but M. Simon mentions three
principal houses of this kind, and alludes to others.
Adult workwomen are also received, being bound
for eighteen months.   The moral advantages of the
surveillance exercised over the girls is apparent in
the fact that they are more readily sought in
marriage by respectable workmen than girls apprenticed in Lyons ; yet the gathering together of
numbers is surely, in itself, to be regretted, as
paving the way for the adoption of the same principle for the mere sake of economical advantage.
While families, however, eagerly seek the shelter
for their daughters, the masters make no profits,
because they are conducting business in a manner
at variance with the habits of the surrounding

trade ; which instantly retrenches in an unfavourable season in a way which is impossible to a
great establishment with an expensive plant.

The very same idea was being in the year 1861
carried out on a small scale in the French colony
of Algiers for the first time. As I was an eye-
witness of its commencement, in the month of
January of that year, it may be of use for me to re-
late in what way— half-economical, half-charitable—
the germ of a vast system of female industry may
spring up. About three miles from the town of
Algiers is a ravine of the most beautiful and ro-
mantic description, called from some local tradition *La Femme Sauvage.* It winds about among
the steep hills, its sides clothed with the pine, the
ilex, the olive, and with an underwood of infinite
variety and loveliness. Wild flowers grow there in
rich profusion, and under the bright blue sky of
that almost tropical climate it seems as if anything
so artificial and unnatural as our systems of industry could hardly exist for shame ; yet in that
very valley young female children were winding
silk for twelve clear hours a day !

The conditions of the case were as follows :—

Considerably nearer the town is a large orphanage, containing about four hundred children, under the care of the sisters of St Vincent de Paul. Many of them are half-castes, others the poorest dregs as it were of the French population ; and they are exactly the same material as in England or Ireland would be drifted into workhouses. Of course, in a place like Algiers, of limited colonial population and resources, it is no easy matter to find a profitable occupation for four hundred orphan girls, and therefore when M. R—— (the very same gentle· man who had organised M. B——'s factory near Lyons) set up a silk-winding mill in *La Femme Sauvage*, the Algerine Government, which pays a considerable sum towards the support of the orphanage, were glad to apprentice thirty girls to M. R——, to be bound from the age of thirteen to that of twenty-one, and to work, according to the usual conditions of French industry, twelve hours a day. The work consisted in winding the raw silk from the cocoon, by hand, aided by a slight machinery, and then in another part of the factory spinning it by means of the ordinary apparatus into skeins of silk ready for the market of the

Lyons weavers. Three Sisters of Charity accompanied the children, and were to superintend them at all times, in the dormitory, the dining-room, and on Sundays, their only day of recreation. When the thirty apprentices were duly trained, M. R—— intended to take seventy more, who were also to be accompanied by their devoted superintendents; so that he purposed to have one hundred girls steadily training in that secluded valley, a thousand miles from here, the forerunners of a social change which might gradually develop Algiers into a manufacturing country, and absorb the lives of an untold number of women. I attended the little fete of installation, when a high ecclesiastical dignitary of Algiers came to perform divine service at the little chapel on the premises; he was accompanied by several of the civic functionaries of the town, whose carriages stood in the ravine, making quite a festive bustle. The two partners were gay and smiling—indeed, I believe them to have been good men, delighted not merely with the business aspects but with the benevolent side of their scheme; the sisters were radiantly pleased with the prospects of their charges; the dormitories were airy and whole

some, the dining-room and kitchen clean and com-
modious. The hundred girls, after being taught a
respectable trade, and enjoying careful moral superintendence during their youthful years, would
be free at twenty-one, and would probably find
respectable marriages without difficulty. Things
being as they are in this modern life of ours, it was
undoubtedly a good and kind scheme, well and
carefully planned ; careful for the welfare of the
children in this world and the next ; and yet, perhaps, you will not wonder that I could not help
thinking of those poor children at their eternal
spinnings whenever, in after spring days, I walked
over the wild hills and through the scented glens
of Algiers ; and that they brought home to me,
from the vivid contrast of the untrammelled nature
around me, what perhaps in Europe might never
strike the heart with equal vividness, that our
modern civilisation is in some respects a very singular thing, when the kind hearts of a great nation
can best show their kindness to orphan girls by
shutting them up to spin silk at a machine for
twelve hours a day from the age of thirteen to that
of twenty-one.

Eight years of youthful girlhood with the smallest possibility during that time of sewing, cooking,
sweeping, dusting, and with neither play nor instruction except the little they can pick up on
Sunday. What would they be like in the year
1869!

So much for silk at Lyons and Algiers ; and remembering that at Lyons the mode of industry is
as yet very favourable to women, let us see how
matters stand in regard to cotton and woollen at
Rouen and at Lille, where, as a rule, the system of
large factories already prevails. Referring to M.
Simon's book we find that he starts on the first
page of his preface with stating that he has passed
more than a year in visiting the principal centres
of industry in France, and that whereas the workman was once an intelligent force, he is now only
an intelligence directing a force—that of steam ;
and that the immediate consequence of the change
has been to replace men by women, because
women are cheaper, and can direct the steam force
with equal efficiency. " A few years ago," says he,
" we had very little mechanical weaving, and, so to
speak, no spinning by machinery ; now, France

has definitely and gloriously taken her place among the countries of large production," (*la grande industrie.*) He speaks of the men gathered together in regiments of labour presenting a firm and serried face to the powers of the State, no longer needing a rallying cry of opposition, since they are in mutual intercourse for twelve hours a day. "And what," he asks, "shall we say of the women? Formerly isolated in their households, now herded together in manufactories. When Colbert, the Minister of Louis XIV., was seeking how to regenerate the agricultural and industrial resources of France, he wished to collect the women into workshops, foreseeing the pecuniary advantages of such a concentration, but even his all-powerful will failed to accomplish this end ; and France, which loves to live under a system of rigid administration, makes an exception in favour of domestic life, and would fain feel itself independent within four walls. But that which Colbert failed to achieve, even with the help of Louis the Great, a far more powerful monarch has succeeded in bringing to pass. From the moment when steam appeared in the industrial world, the wheel, the spindle, and the distaff broke

in the hand, and the spinsters and weavers, deprived of their ancient livelihood, fled to the
shadow of the tall factory chimney." "The
mothers," says M. Simon, "have left the hearth
and the cradle, and the young girls and the little
children themselves have run to offer their feeble
arms ; whole villages are silent, while huge brick
buildings swallow up thousands of living humanity
from dawn of day until twilight shades."

Need I say more, except to point out that when
once any new social or industrial principle has, so
to speak, fairly set in, the last remains of the old
system stand their ground with extreme difficulty
against the advancing tide, and that trades by which
solitary workers can earn a sufficient livelihood are
every day decreasing in value, or being swept off
into *la grande industrie.* Sewing will assuredly all
be wrought in factories before long ; the silk work,
which formerly stretched down the valley of the
Rhone as far as Avignon, has gradually drawn up
to Lyons, leaving the city of the Popes empty and
desolate within its vast walls. At Dijon, M. Maitre
has gathered up the leather work of that ancient
capital into his admirably organised *ateliers,* where

C

he employs two hundred men and one hundred women, and binds prayer-books and photographic albums and *porte-monnaies* enough to supply an immense retail trade in Paris. In England it is the same : we gather our people together and together, we cheapen and cheapen that which we produce. Did you ever, when children, play with quicksilver, and watch the tiny glittering balls attracted in larger and larger globules until they all rolled together into one ? Such is the law of modern industry in England and France, and in all other countries according as they follow the lead of these two nations in the theoretic principles of life which lead to those results which are at once the triumph and the dark side of modern civilisation.

Having thus pointed out the conditions under which so large a proportion of our national commercial prosperity is carried on, permit me to say a few words regarding the practical consequences and duties it entails. Nobody can doubt that so vast a social change must be gradually inducing an equally great moral change, and that some of the consequences must be bad. I am careful to limit my expressions, because it must not be forgotten

that I am not speaking of the poor or of the degraded, but of the bulk of the factory workpeople
of England and France, and of large classes in
Scotland and Ireland, who earn their bread by
respectable industry, and are often the main support of their families. It is true that I have heard
and could tell grievous stories of the wild, half-
savage state of the women and girls in some districts, in some factories, under some bad or careless
masters ; but that is not the side of things to which
I wish to draw attention :—it is rather to the *inevitable* results of non-domestic labour for women,
and to the special duties it imposes on those of
a higher class. In the first place, there are the
obvious results of the absence of married women
from their homes,—an absence which I believe we
may fairly state should, in the majority of instances,
be discouraged by every possible moral means,
since the workman must be very wretched indeed
before his wife's absence can be a source of real
gain. Then there is the utter want of domestic
teaching and training during the most important
years of youth. How to help this is no easy
matter, since, whatever we may do in regard to

married women, we certainly cannot prevent girls
from being employed in factories, nor, in the present state of civilisation, provide other work for
them if we could so prevent them. And lastly,
there is what I believe to be the sure deterioration
of health. We are as yet only in the second generation; but any one who has closely watched the
effect of ten hours in England and twelve hours in
France, of labour chiefly conducted in a standing
posture, amidst the noise, and, in some cases, the
necessary heat of factories, upon young growing
girls, knows how the weakly ones are carried off by
consumption, or any hereditary morbid tendency,
and what the subtle nervous strain must be upon all.

Truly, there is enough in the necessary, and what
we have come to consider the natural, features of
modern industry, to arouse the earnest conscientious attention of the wives and daughters of employers, and of all good women whom Providence
has gifted with education and means. And as
the need is peculiar, so must the help be. Except
in some isolated cases, we will hope and believe
that it is not, strictly speaking, missionary work.
It is not to teach the wholly uneducated, to reclaim

the drunkard, to rouse the sinner ; there is enough of that to be done in England and France, but it is not of that I am speaking. Help, and teaching, and friendliness are wanting for the respectable workwoman, such as have already been partly provided for the respectable workman.

But I will not pursue this theme further. What I wished to prove by reference to admitted facts was the absorption of women into non-domestic industry,—a change which is taking place not in the mechanical departments alone, and which, if society does not restrain, it should endeavour to organise, or at least to ensure that the remains of its own ancient organisation does not complicate by cruel difficulties and restrictions.

We now come to the real grievance of which our countrywomen may very justly complain, and which I do not believe to have reached anything like the same importance in France, nor as yet in America. It is this—that while the prevailing tendency of our time is to draw women out of domestic life, it is a purely economical and selfish tendency, acting by competition alone, and casting aside unprofitable material. Women are more and more

left to provide for themselves, and society takes
hardly any trouble to enable them to do so, either
by education or by opening the doors to salaried
employment. The great overplus of the female
sex in England, caused chiefly by the wholesale
emigration of men to the colonies, increases the
difficulty tenfold ; and except in the mere mechanical trades, where numbers rather than skill are in
demand, it is exceedingly difficult for them to find
anything to do.

In fact, the general freedom and *laisser aller* of
English political and social life, while it serves
many admirable purposes in the general economy
of the nation, allows the weaker classes, those who
are in any way unfitted for the race, to go to the
wall, while the others pass by. I believe the *very
poor* to suffer far more in England than elsewhere ;
and I am sure there is no country on earth where
so many women are allowed to drift helplessly
about, picking up the scanty bread of insufficient
earnings. We are at present in an extraordinary
state of social disorganisation. Much of the old
order has passed away, under the overwhelming
pressure of modern ideas, of the development of

the mechanical arts, of the increase of numbers.
There is no use in lamenting over it, beyond the
occasional expression of a personal preference for
the simpler forms of the olden time. The change
must be accepted, and whatever evils it has produced had best be fairly investigated with a view
to find a remedy. On this ground I think women
are fairly entitled to utter a very vigorous complaint; on this ground I sympathise with every
effort to train them to mechanical crafts; on this
ground I think we have a right to ask that society, which is no longer able or willing to provide for women in the old-fashioned way, should
try to give them an equal chance with men in
providing for themselves. This chance is now
only equal upon the lowest level. In mere handi-
craft of an unskilled kind, provided that no great
strength is required, the woman has perhaps even
a better prospect of employment, because she will
work for less wages. But the idea that she may
fairly be left to provide for herself has spread in
other grades; and there, just where comparative
degrees of education and refinement have made
her needs greater, factory wages seem alone at her

command. I purpose in the following pages to
pass in review the different remedies which have
been suggested and partly worked out on a small
scale, taking the economical question as a basis,
but not refraining from expressing strong convictions when my subject touches, as it must often
do, upon those moral considerations which are of
infinitely greater importance than worldly prosperity, or even competency.   If obliged to make
so painful a choice, I would say for the numbers
what I would say for the individual,—that it is
better to be starved in body than made worse in the
moral and spiritual life.   I would wish for my sex
what I would wish for my sister.   By this standard
I should judge every scheme for the improving of
the position of women ; and if any of my readers
deem that I have used an exaggerated expression,
they will be mindful how impossible it is to treat
of even a practical, and, as I trust, a temporary
theme, without appealing to those religious faiths
and moral convictions, which, whether by their
presence or their absence, must necessarily and
deeply influence our judgment on all social questions such as these.

II.

THE CHANGES OF EIGHTY
YEARS.

THE CHANGES OF EIGHTY YEARS.

TOWARDS the end of the last century, when new theories of social life circulated in all circles, from the very courts of the most autocratic monarchs down to the literary middle-class, and in some countries to the lowest population, it was to be expected that women would both interest themselves in, and form the subject of, various opinions incident to the epoch. Rousseau was the apostle of one school of thought; but there is little evidence that his vigorous, ardent, but strangely twisted mind ever deeply affected this country. Here and there might be found an enthusiastic father, who, accepting part of his teaching, would insist on his children running barefoot and living according to the light of nature. But the more sentimental and questionable parts of Rousseau's philosophy found

little favour here. Even the English writer of
the last century, who might be generally supposed
to have imbibed something of his doctrines, speaks
with contempt of "Rousseau's wild chimeras" in
regard to education, and with strong indignation
of the corrupting tendency of his opinions on the
education of girls, and appeals forcibly, not exactly
to the Christian ideal, but to a sort of high
Spartan virtue, which the benevolent minds of
those days had convinced themselves to be possible of attainment, if only boys and girls could
be trained from infancy according to its maxims.
This notion that the root of all evil lay in bad
primary education, was the predominant fixed
idea of that day. "Harry and Lucy" and "Frank"
were written to illustrate it, by Maria Edgeworth;
and her father spent a long life in the teaching
and training of his numerous offspring, with a sort
of implicit confidence in the result which enhances
the pathos of that tablet in the little church at
Edgeworthstown, which records the deaths of
four youths ·in opening manhood. Four of those
young creatures who were to inaugurate that golden
age of sense and virtue were cut off in the spring-

time of their promise; and a sister's hand records
their names and ages, with the simple ejaculation,
" Alas, my brothers ! " The author of " Sandford
and Merton," another of the benevolent and philosophical minds of the last century tried to educate
a young girl to be his future wife; and the story of
his mishaps is so amusing, and so illustrative of
the tone of thought which ruled the most enlightened circles of the time, that it is worth recording
here as an anecdote extremely pertinent to our
subject.

Mr Thomas Day, born in 1748, was educated at
the Charter House and at Oxford; and, on his
coming of age, inherited a fortune of £1200 a
year. At an early period he manifested a particular
fondness for scrutinising human character ; and at
eighteen he took a journey into Wales that he might
observe the natives, who, " as still treading the un-
improved paths of nature, might be presumed to
have the qualities of the mind pure, and unsophis-
ticated by art."

While still quite young he fell in love with a
lady who rejected his addresses ; and as he forth-
with despaired of finding another woman who

could fulfil his dreams, he determined to educate
one for the purpose. He was one-and-twenty when,
in pursuance of this remarkable scheme, he went to
Shrewsbury, accompanied by a barrister, Mr Bick-
nell, and explored the Foundling Hospital, whence
he selected two girls of twelve years old, both
beautiful, one a blonde, whom he called Lucretia,
the other a clear auburn brunette, dignified with
the lovely and poetic name of Sabrina. Mr Day,
who, in spite of his oddities, was an excellent man, was intrusted with these two children,
on certain written conditions, by the governors of
the hospital; and was to choose one to be educated as the future Mrs Day, while the other was
to be apprenticed to a respectable tradeswoman,
and £400 to be paid as a marriage dowry, or to
set her up eventually in business. His selection
was to be made within the year.

The poor gentleman soon found that he had imposed a burden upon himself; his two children
tired and perplexed him; they quarrelled, they
sickened of the small-pox in France, where he had
taken them, without an English servant, that they
might receive no ideas except those which he him-

self might choose to impart. The little girls, however, had their revenge; for when they fell ill they
cried if he left them a minute alone with people
who could not speak English. In eight months
they returned to England; and Mr Day having
decided that Sabrina would grow up most to his
mind, apprenticed Lucretia to a milliner; and she
finally married a linen-draper. He then devoted
himself to make Sabrina a perfect woman; but
none of his experiments had the success he wished.
" Her spirit could not be armed against the dread
of pain and the appearance of danger, a species of
courage which with him was a *sine qua non* in the
character of a wife. When he dropped melted
sealing-wax upon her arms she did not endure it
heroically; nor when he fired pistols at her petti-
coats, which she believed to be charged with balls,
could she refrain from starting aside, or suppress
her screams." He invented secrets, and found she
betrayed them to the servants and her playfellows;
he gave her no rewards, and excluded her from the
knowledge of the value of money, or the admira-
tion bestowed upon beauty; he cut off remorselessly
all the little outward incentives to good behaviour,

leaving her none but that of pleasing him, though
the poor child appears not to have had a notion of
his good intentions; and, of course, "fear had
greatly the ascendant of affection," or, as we should
say, poor little Sabrina became horribly afraid of
him.   At last, falling into despair at his refractory
pupil, he gave up any idea of making her Mrs
Day, and sent her off to a boarding-school, where
she grew up to be " an elegant and amiable " woman.   Mr Day eventually married (at thirty years
of age) a Miss Milner of Yorkshire. He disinter-
estedly settled all her fortune on herself; but his
oddities prevented her money from being of any
use to her.   He made " frequent experiments on
her temper and her attachment;" she had no
carriage, no personal servant, no harpsichord or
music-books; he thought her musical proficiency
" trivial."   He must have worried her in a most
philosophical manner; for we are informed that
though she often wept, she never repined; moreover, she loved him, queer as he was; for her
death, which occurred two years after his own, is
said to have been caused by heartbreak at his
loss.   It was extremely characteristic of Mr Day

that he should have been killed by a kick administered by a favourite foal, which he had
reared, fed, and trained, but which objected to the
bit when its master, " disdaining to employ a horse-
breaker," undertook the task himself.

It is worth while to notice that Day coincided
with certain of Rousseau's opinions about education,
so far as they steered clear of sinfulness ; for he was
a man of strictly virtuous life.   He followed out
with poor little Sabrina the same theory which he
afterwards enforced upon his wife, and which is
thus expressed by the Genevese philosopher :—
" To please, to be useful to us, to make us love
and esteem them, to educate us when young, and
take care of us when grown up, to advise, to con
sole us, to render our lives easy and agreeable,—
these are the duties of women at all times, and
what they should be taught in their infancy.   So
long as we fail to recur to this principle we run
wide of the mark, and all the precepts which are
given them contribute neither to their happiness
nor our own."

This bald abnegation of conscience as the ruling
power never, however, obtained any great currency

D

in England. Although "Sermons to Young Women," and "Letters to my Daughter," sometimes
appeared, which might seem at first sight to preach
the same doctrines, yet through the pages circulated that spirit of loving obedience to a Divine
Master, which is the surest counteractive to all
abasement, and elevates self-sacrifice into a noble
expression of strength.   No trace of this principle
animates the pen of Jean Jacques.   He had a keen
appreciation of the beauty of virtue at times, but
even in this he failed to be consistent, and his
unspiritual nature for ever led him astray even
in his theories.   Rousseau was for ever crying up
" sensibility," as a woman's chief charm and first
requisite ;—" And what," says one of his critics,
" what is sensibility ? Quickness of sensation ; quickness of perception; delicacy.   Thus it is defined by
Dr Johnson ; and the definition gives me no other
idea than of the most exquisitely-polished instinct.
I discern not a trace of the image of God in
either sensation or matter.   Refined seventy times
seven, they are still material ; intellect dwells not
there ; nor will fire ever make lead gold." And
again, the sober tone of English thought on this

subject is well represented by a paragraph in the same work, in which, after dealing with the education of women as part of the race, it is thus continued :—

"When I treat of the peculiar duties of woman, as I should treat of the peculiar duties of a citizen or father, it will be found that I do not mean to insinuate that they should be taken out of their families, speaking of the majority. 'He that hath wife and children,' says Lord Bacon, 'hath given hostages to fortune ; for they are impediments to great enterprises either of virtue or mischief. Certainly the best works, and of greatest merit for the public, have proceeded from the unmarried or childless men.' I say the same of women. But *the welfare of society is not built on extraordinary exertions; and were it more reasonably organised there would be still less need of great abilities and heroic virtues.*"

It appears to me impossible to express facts and principles with greater aptitude and precision than in the above quotation.

I have laid stress upon the great social movement of the last century as being confessedly

the dawn of quite a new order of thought, which
also frequently lapsed into *dis*order, and became
a mere disorganisation and disintegration of the
social system built up in past centuries.   But
whether for good or evil, it was a great upwelling
of life, an upheaving of mental forces, and it had
this new and singular feature that women took
part in every speculation, and even in every
practical effort.   In France, Madame Roland,
Madame de Stael, Madame Recamier, Delphine
Gay, marked the new era, culminating as it were
in the stormy and brilliant intellect of Madame
Dudevant.   In England we had Maria Edgeworth, Jane Austen, and a host of lesser names.
The extraordinary literary popularity achieved by
such a writer as Mrs Hemans was in itself quite a
new thing.   We possess a great number of memoirs, such as those of Mrs Trench and Mary
Leadbeater, of Hannah More and Elizabeth Fry,
which show how worthily Englishwomen could
speak, write, and act in the semi-domestic circles
these inhabited.   My impression on reading the
biographies of both sexes, dating in the two generations previous to our own, is that a very great

change in the education and ideas of women gradually developed after the year 1780. Very few might choose to follow continental theories, but they made a certain impression nevertheless, as may be especially noted in the account given by Mrs Schimmelpenninck of the education bestowed upon her in her early youth.

Within the last forty years we have seen a still more remarkable change. The mechanical improvements which have tended to make life so much easier, the diffusion of education, the facile access to books, and the rise of periodical literature, all these things have caused innumerable women to come forward into activity. The average power displayed, I believe to have been highly respectable ; here and there women were found capable of thorough good work, though their advantages of a technical kind were always much less than they might be. But the uprising was almost wholly unconscious and spontaneous, and as such was the more dignified and desirable. I believe it might for ever have remained so, to the great satisfaction of the numerous public who would let women do almost anything " if only they would not talk about it." But in prevention of this silent growth arose the great difficulty of which I spoke at length in the last chapter. The emigration of men, the creation of the factory system, the disruption from numerous causes of the simple old life,—simple, kindly, and in many instances coarse,—depicted in the novels of the last century, threw numbers of women on their own resources. Then began the cry for equal advantages, equal education. The slow process of natural development was too tardy for the pressing need. Take up a book of a hundred years ago, and where do you find the women struggling alone. Here and there a "young gentlewoman" is companion or maid to a great lady, and ends by making a splendid match. But take up a novel of the present day, and you are pretty sure to find traces of the new feature in our society, even if the heroine be not a fox-like Becky Sharpe, or a passionate and yet austere Jane Eyre.

I do not say that here and there we should not in any case have had a few vigorous intellects exerting themselves on the problems of social life, and even pushing the claim of equality to an

extreme. But except for the material need which
exerted a constant pressure over a large and educated class, the " woman's movement " could never
have become in England a subject of popular
comment, and to a certain extent of popular sympathy. In this short sketch I have given the main
outline of my subject up to the immediate changes
of the last ten years, and I would point out that
these originally took their rise in the question of
earnings. I will rapidly enumerate them, returning
in separate chapters to each section which demands
a detailed notice.

Ten years ago, although there was an earnest
and active group of people deeply interested in all
that relates to female education and industry, and
to the reform of the laws affecting the property of
married women, and though efforts were being made
in many directions for the bettering of the condition
of the mass of single women in this country, there
was no centre of meeting, nor any one work which
could be said to draw together the names of the
ladies so actively employed. But the separate exertions carried on were surely and solidly laying the
foundations of what has now taken its place as one

of the chief social "movements" of the day. In education, a great start was made by the erection of the "Ladies' Colleges." Both at the one located in Harley Street, and at the one carried on in Bedford Square, under the auspices of a most generous and indefatigable foundress, the girl pupils were brought in contact with the minds of several eminent professors of the day. The whole standard of female education in regard to history, the dead and living languages, mathematics, and musical science, was changed. The pupils were made to understand what is knowledge and what is not, and to appreciate as well as to acquire.

In literature many women had achieved a solid reputation, among whom perhaps Miss Martineau took the first place, from the number and practical nature of her forcible writings; and one other mind, deep, thoughtful, and sincere, had been frequently attracted away from the more intellectual and artistic pursuits in which it was chiefly distinguished, towards the problems of woman's life and work—I refer to Mrs Jameson. The oftener I recur to those former years, and to the thoughts and plans current among the younger generation

of my sex, the greater is, I feel, our debt of gratitude to her for the influence she exerted, not only
in her writings, but in her own person.   She was
ever ready to give time, thought, and her best
judgment to the plans of her younger friends ; and
her long experience of life, and strong sense of
religious and social morality, acted as a firm re-
straint against all antisocial theories, such as have
occasionally been started, *apropos* of these questions, in other countries.   She was thoroughly
liberal, widely cultivated, not at all cowardly as to
the trying of experiments, (such as the medical
career,) but she always appeared to act from some
inner law of womanhood, which it was impossible
for her to infringe, and which imparted grace and
consistency to everything she said and did.

The department of intellectual activity in which
she naturally took most interest was that of the
artist ; and a group of young women, who pursued
art in one or other of its various branches, were
among her constant visitors during her sojourns
in London.   It was, however, to all the problems
connected with the care of the sick and the relief
of the poor that her thoughts chiefly turned, in

those intervals of leisure left by her own works on
historical art. Her pursuits had led her to a
lengthened residence in various continental cities,
and she had investigated with zeal and care the
institutions which are there so deeply rooted, and
which may be said to supply the place of our poor-
law. The result in her mind was a strong belief in
the efficiency of sisterhoods ; and she embodied her
opinions in two admirable lectures, entitled " Sisters of Charity," and "The Communion of Labour,"
which were personally delivered in the drawing-
rooms of two lady friends, and afterwards reprinted
by Longman. To these were finally appended her
admirable " Letter to Lord John Russell," in which
she touches on many wants suffered by her countrywomen, and devotes some pages to the consideration of the medical question. This letter is
one of the most remarkable productions of Mrs
Jameson's pen. It is characterised by a simplicity
and dignity which reveal the aged and experienced
woman, willing to come forward and stake her
well-won reputation for the sake of those younger
than herself ; it is written alike without heat and
without timidity, and is a noble example. of that

style of writing in which the moral character of the author penetrates every sentence, and infuses an authority to which mere eloquence could never attain.

The general movement had attained the level I have attempted to describe, when a bill was intro-duced into Parliament for securing the earnings of married women to their own discretionary use. It was presented in the Upper House by Lord Brougham, and in the Lower by Sir Erskine Perry. The long list of signatures was headed by the names of Anna Jameson and Mary Howitt, fol-lowed by numerous signatures of eminent women, among them that of Elizabeth Barrett Browning. In its immediate object this effort failed.   The bill was not carried ; but it undoubtedly exercised a strong influence in that clause of the ensuing Di-vorce Bill, which secures to *deserted wives* the use of their own earnings for themselves and their fami-lies ; and in so doing, helped to prevent the recur-rence of all the worst cases of misfortune resulting from the law ; for whatever may be considered the abstract justice of the case, it was in cases of deser-tion or cruelty, when the husband, returning, swept

off at a blow the hard-accumulated earnings of his
wife for her family, that bitter injustice chiefly
resulted. Such cases are now under legal protection.

But this, though fairly to be laid to its credit,
was far from the only effect of the defeated bill.
It induced, throughout the spring and early summer
of 1856, a lively discussion in the newspapers ; and
though ridicule was, in some instances, poured on
its supporters, much real, warm, lasting sympathy
was elicited, and many men came forward to give
their help. Even more important was it that, in
the effort to obtain signatures, people interested in
the question were brought into communication in
all parts of the kingdom, and that the germs of an
effective movement were scattered far and wide.
It is an act of justice to recall, that the first idea
of this bill was due to Miss Leigh Smith, now
Madame Bodichon, a lady since her marriage ab-
sent from England during the greater part of each
year, but who has been, from first to last, an unfail-
ing friend to the cause. Much of the subsequent
work was greatly aided by the generous help of Mr
George Hastings.

It was some six months later, in October 1856, that a stray number of a periodical, professing to be edited by ladies, caught my eye in the window of a small shop in Edinburgh. On making some inquiries at the office, I found it to be a paper of a very harmless but very inefficient sort. The proprietor, however, wished to improve it ; made an offer, after some negotiation, of the entire control of this periodical ; and then it was that I asked Mrs Jameson's advice as to the desirability of attempting to devote such a magazine to the special objects of woman's work. She entered into the point with her usual sympathetic kindness, and gave her advice in the affirmative. Thereupon Madame Bodichon placed in the hands of an experienced friend a considerable sum of money, to be applied to the improvement, and, if desirable, the purchase of the magazine. Negotiations with the proprietor were entered into, which, however, proved unsatisfactory ; and we were advised not to spend money and effort over a property which did not appear to be worth either, but to start afresh, with a new journal of our own, in London. It took some months to arrange our plans; but in March 1858 the *English Woman's Journal* was commenced, under two joint editors; the necessary money having been collected from various good friends to the cause, in the form of shares in a limited liability company. Seven years elapsed, during which seventy-eight numbers were issued, at a cost of anxiety and responsibility far beyond what any merely literary journal could entail, inasmuch as the subject-matter of this particular periodical touched at all points upon the dearest interests and safeguards of civilised society, was partially connected with the religious views of various bodies of Christians, and presented in other directions a perfect pitfall of ridicule, ever ready to open beneath the feet of the conductors.

At the seventy-eighth number, a junction was effected with another magazine, and the journal still exists in an amalgamated form.

It now needs to be considered in what relation this journal could be expected to stand to the rest of the periodical press. Had it from the first any hope, any expectation, any *wish* to come forward in the same field with the able monthlies which contained the best writing of the day? To this question an emphatic *No* must at once be given. Such an idea would have been perfectly hopeless and absurd, and indeed self-destructive ; for a subject cannot be at once popular and unpopular, rich and poor, clothed in purple and fine linen, and undergoing incessant fear of a social martyrdom. If it had been wished to start a brilliant and successful magazine, some eminent publisher should have been secured, and persuaded to undertake active pecuniary interest and risk ; all the best known female writers should have been engaged, " regardless of expense ;" *and then*—good-bye to the advocacy of any subject which would have entailed a breath of ridicule ; good-bye to any thorough expression of opinion ; good-bye to the humble but ceaseless struggle of all these years, and to the results which have sprung up around the small office where so many workers collected together, because the purpose and the plan were *honestly conceived and carried out.*

A few dates and details as to the different practical branches of the movement may not be out of place, in connexion with this slight sketch of the history of the journal. The first of those who

joined the early work was Miss Maria Rye. At
the time of the proposed introduction of a bill on
the property of married women, our attention was
attracted by an excellent article on the subject
signed M. S. R. An inquiry made of the editor
was answered by a visit from the writer, then
living near London with her family, and.devoting
her leisure to literature. From that time she became the fast friend of her fellow-workers; and
when it became necessary to engage a secretary to
manage the large amount of correspondence which
the bill entailed, Miss Rye became that secretary,
and was immediately brought in contact with its
supporters, many of whom were men of eminence.
In the summer of 1857, Miss Craig first came from
Edinburgh, and became assistant secretary to the
National Association for the Promotion of Social
Science, then in the course of formation. In June
1859, Miss Boucherett came to London, desirous
of organising the Society for Promoting the Employment of Women, and found in the same office
many friends and helpers. The infant society was
finally organised in connexion with the Social
Science Association.

It was now, in the winter of 1859-60, that the group of works, which have since been frequently reviewed by the press, took their rise, all of them in a certain way linked to the society founded by Miss Boucherett, except the Victoria Press, which was undertaken on a separate basis, aided by friends who had for many years desired to see women employed in printing. At the same time a law-copying office was started by the Society, and Miss Rye installed as manager; and Miss Boucherett herself undertook the direct superintendence of a middle-class school intended to fit young women for taking situations as bookkeepers, cashiers, and clerks.

A register was likewise formally opened at the office of the Society, and absorbed into itself a small register previously kept in the office of the *Journal;* but as the two offices were at this time brought under one roof, at 19 Langham Place, the register work has since been carried on, almost without distinction, in either room.

The reading room, which had been started over the little office which the *Journal* originally inhabited in Prince's Street, Cavendish Square, was at the same time moved into the same large house,

E

secured, by the munificence of one lady, for the
three institutions, and where they have now remained for four years.

The emigration movement, in which Miss Rye's
name has lately become prominent, grew naturally
and imperceptibly out of the work of the law-
copying office. So many women applied for employment, to whom it was impossible to give it,
that Miss Rye tried to assist some of them to emi-
grate. One by one was thus helped with a little
money, lent by friends for the purpose, and furnished with letters of introduction. Little by little
her time became absorbed by constant claims of
the kind. The law-copying business was carried
on under a forewoman, and Miss Rye gave herself
up to the assisting of emigrants, and at last determined on taking a voyage to our colonies in one
of the emigration ships, that she might herself
investigate the condition of the labour market, and
the best means for supplying needs at home and
abroad. Miss Jane Lewin has been Miss Rye's
associate in the work from the first, and now su-
perintends the Middle-class Emigration Society at
12 Portugal Street, W.C.

The last point of interest in the movement is the experimental examination of girls, conducted by the examiners of the University of Cambridge, which took place the first week of December 1863, at which upwards of ninety students presented themselves, and which may ultimately lead to the full opening of the examinations of both universities.

In this general outline no mention has been made of the many, many kind friends and helpers who have encircled us with help and sympathy from the first, and who have been the main stay of those whose names happened to become more prominent. There is no possibility of recording the manifold acts of help and kindness which have taken place on all sides; and when I look back over these years, and compare the conditions of success with the plans which floated before our inexperienced eyes at the beginning, I am doubly impressed with the power of individual character and individual effort. In this sort of work, as in commercial barter, an adequate price must be paid down for every result. "Though the mills of God grind slowly, yet they grind exceeding small," says

Longfellow, translating from a German poet; and whoso wishes to achieve any lasting good, however small in quantity or humble in kind, must pay down true coin, of motive and practice, of outline and of detail.

This is the more imperative, because, in any purely secular work, it is next to impossible to secure those peculiar benefits which spring from thorough organisation, by which the weak are sustained, the idle stimulated, the unsteady held in check. Any twenty people will obey a common religious authority, and they will obey the law of the land, when it enforces measures for its own defence, (as in the army and navy,) or when it enforces the fulfilment of contracts, as in the different relations of master and workman. But when simple benevolent work is in question, which is carried on, neither by the direct authority of a religious body, nor by the principle of pecuniary contracts, it is next to impossible to combine a number of people in any reasonably permanent or satisfactory manner. There is a want of organic coherence in the elements of human character, and this is why the best workers are apt to lament the

difficulties of working through committees, even
when these committees are formed of really sympa-
thising people. Then it is that the personal worth
of every individual tells conspicuously upon the
matter in hand ; or rather we may say, that *without*
personal worthiness there is really no achievement
at all. Societies and committees have no inherent
aptitude in getting through work ; indeed, it may
be doubted whether some of the *momentum* is not
actually lost in the friction they entail. Their
great use is in offering a guarantee for the funds
subscribed by the public ; the wisdom of the re-
distribution is purely according to the honesty and
the energy of the individual members to whom any
branch is committed. A flaw in the instrument is
a flaw in the result, to a much greater extent than
in the working out of a system. Among the hundreds of thousands of Wesleyan Methodists, all
backing each other up by that mighty power of
religious communion, the inferior capacity, the
slacker zeal, of some members, are hardly visible,
being so intimately blended with the common stock.
But let none argue thus in choosing helpers for a
secular work ; such work lacks the fusing element,

and each atom stands out, hard or soft, round or square, crooked or straight, as the case may be. Even worth will hardly save weakness, and strength carries its own ends in lower spheres. To those who watch with yearning anxiety the progress of a movement like ours, the great source of hope and cheerfulness lies in the attainment of a thorough conviction that, however much it may fail in rounded unity of action, no effort, no thought, no single, true, unselfish exertion of one for another, amidst all the many people gathered together in its progress, has been in vain.

III.

EDUCATED DESTITUTION.

EDUCATED DESTITUTION.

CCORDING to the different constitution
of different minds, will be the relative
importance attached to problems affecting the many or the few. It may reasonably be
urged that penniless women in the upper classes,
though *comparatively* few in number, are more important than the mass of their working fellow-
countrywomen, because of their superior influence
on the future. In this chapter we will exclusively
consider the case of ladies who have to earn their
own living.

The proportion of the entire upper and middle
classes to the lower is in itself but small ; most
people would be surprised to realise *how* small,
for, taken together, the two first do not number
half the latter, nor consequently a third of the
whole population. It has been roughly calculated

that the middle ranks are about three times as
numerous as the aristocratic, and that the working
classes are about three times as numerous as the
middle ranks ; or in other words, of thirteen units,
one would represent the aristocracy, *three* the middle ranks, and the remaining *nine* stand for the
" masses." So that four parts out of thirteen are
all with which I now mean to deal ; and of this proportion only the female members ; and of these again
only that section which has to gain its daily bread.

How large is that section? Let us inquire.
Everybody will at once admit that the theory
of civilised life in this and all other countries,
not excluding the democratic States of America,
is that the women of the upper and middle
classes are supported by their male relatives :
daughters by their fathers, wives by their husbands.
If a lady has to work for her livelihood, it is universally considered to be a misfortune, an exception to the ordinary rule. All good fathers wish
to provide for their daughters ; all good husbands
think it their bounden duty to keep their wives.
All our laws are framed strictly in accordance with
this hypothesis ; and all our social customs adhere

to it more strictly still. We make no room in our social framework for any other idea, and in no moral or practical sphere do the exceptions more lamentably and thoroughly prove the rule. Women of the lower class may work, *must* work, in the house, if not out of it—too often out of it! But among us, it is judged best to carefully train the woman as the moraliser, the refiner, the spiritual element.

There is little or nothing to be urged against it, if it were practicable in action. It may be that the benefit conferred on society by a class of tender, refined, thoughtful women, secluded from its rougher paths and grosser problems, is inestimable. We can hardly imagine what a civilised country would be like without such a class of women, for they have existed in all ages enriched by the higher forms of literature and art. The benefit they confer does now largely exist in certain directions, and might under certain moral conditions be realised for the whole upper and middle classes, if the theory of a material provision for all educated women were humanly possible, *which it is not.*

It is not possible! Let us not forget this. Educated women must work for money. It is no fault
to be obliged to assert this, nor to be compelled
to believe it. Our theory and our practice are
wide apart in this matter, and the cause of the discrepancy is as deep as the cause of strikes or commercial crises; nay, deeper still, as the cause of
misfortune, improvidence, or crime in human
nature.

The aristocracy are rich enough to make some
invariable, though scanty, provision for their female members, but the middle class is at the
mercy of a thousand accidents of commercial or
professional life, and thousands and thousands of
destitute educated women have to earn their daily
bread. Probably every reader has a female relative or intimate friend whom trade-failures, the
exigencies of a numerous household, or the early
death of husband or father, has compelled to this
course; it is in the experience of every family.
Most of these ladies take to teaching. The reports of the Governesses' Benevolent Institution
reckon fifteen thousand governesses as an item in
our population.

As in natural sciences the discovery of great
laws is constantly inaugurated by minute observation of particular facts, let us leave the census
alone, and try to examine one family, the type of
many thousands. The father, by his labour of
head and hand, gains sufficient to support his wife,
and say three children, one of whom is a girl.
The father will certainly send his two boys to
school, whether it be to a twopenny, or to an expensive boarding-school: the girl will probably be
sent also for a few years to one much inferior ; but
if there is work to be done at home she will be
kept at home to do it. In the middle-class family
we have taken as a type, she is much employed in
making shirts for her two school-boy brothers.
We have heard of a case in which some young
ladies, who were offered gratuitous instruction in
one of the best ladies' colleges, were kept at home
for that purpose. Her learning is not insisted on,
while her brothers are urged forward, and every
facility given for them to pursue their studies at
home. When the girl is fourteen or fifteen, we
shall certainly find her taken away from school, if
not earlier ; while the boys proceed to some higher

place of instruction, or begin to learn a profession. But now that the daughter is permanently under his roof, perhaps the father, who depends entirely on his yearly income, may begin to have some little anxiety as to her future. Perhaps he may ardently wish for an instant that he could leave her an assured livelihood, or a means of gaining one. He balances in his mind the expense of training her as a first-rate governess; but this would be very great, and he has not courage or energy to look for any exceptional work for his young daughter; he would not make her a clerk or a nurse. So he silences all anxiety for the future, by saying, " She will marry: indeed it would be a very bad speculation, a very foolish outlay of money, to give her a trade or profession ; she may never want it, and her brothers are sure to want all the money I can spare." Plausible but fearful logic. It is true that the *chances* are on the side of her marrying, so it is not astonishing that an ordinary father trusts to them; yet the miseries which befall a penniless woman are so great, that if the opposing chance were but as one in a hundred, the parent should provide against it.

It is of this material that our forlorn single
women are made : thousands utterly destitute save
for charity ; thousands more who, insufficiently provided for, eke out a miserable income by rigid and
painful economy. We may lay it down as a primary
social law, conceded by all political economists,
that a father ought to provide for all his children, or
give them the means of providing for themselves.
For their sons they perform this duty with anxious
care ; but for their daughters they neglect it, because they hope and expect that some one else
will do it for them. This is the plain state of the
case ; this *expectation* is in innumerable instances a
daughter's *provision*.

But there is another reason why the father con-
fides his daughter's future so wholly to her possible
husband : women are so unused to have or to
hold property, and the law throws the gifts or the
earnings of a married woman so completely into
her husband's power, that the father is little
tempted to save up his money to give to another
man ; nor to train up his daughter expensively,
when another man has legal power over the fruits
of her education, and can take away any money

she earns. Women have so little individuality in
the eyes of most men, that when a parent has
married his girl he feels to have washed his hands
of all responsibility about her, and of course in her
youth he looks forward to the chances of being
able so to cast his burden on another. But surely
in the present state of England, and even under
the present state of the law in regard to the property and earnings of married women, there is a
sort of madness in trusting to such a slender reed.
The daughter may marry, but her husband may
die, or fail, or be too poor to support her and her
children ; let her at least be trained beforehand to
some possible way of getting her bread.

And suppose this girl, whom we took as a type,
does not marry, and is left penniless and single
by the death of her father. What can she do?
She is untrained ; she cannot be a good governess;
she cannot undertake to teach in a national school;
and her father taught her no trade, and gave her
no money with which to start.

I can conceive of no more desperate and dreadful case than this ; for the workhouse, or other
charitable asylum, which may in some sort supply

the wants of the poor, are a cruel degradation to such an one. How fearfully common it is, is proved by the reports of the institution to which I have alluded. It is, indeed, almost impossible to make a clear division between this chapter and the next ; for the profession of the teacher has been, as it were, the open gulph into which the whole class of which we speak have until very lately rushed, and the story of a destitute lady is almost synonymous with that of a destitute teacher. Inasmuch, however, as other paths are beginning to be opened, it seemed well to consider the general question of poverty among educated women first. The *causes* attach to the moral responsibility of parents, especially fathers. Remedies are hard to seek, and an ounce of prevention is worth a pound of cure. It is lamentable to think how small a proportion of our population insures, when it is so cheap, easy, and safe for the *young* married man to do so, and creates help for the women of a family just when, by the death of the bread-winner, they would otherwise be left without resource. To insure, or to save up a small portion for every female child, this is a father's sacred duty. Style, position, the keeping

F

of many servants, all should be stinted to effect
this end. Better bring up a girl to help in the
household work, and leave her a modest provision
in future years, than keep two housemaids, bring
her up " with her hands before her," and leave
her without a halfpenny. There are large classes
of poor mercantile and professional men for whom
this is exactly the question : " Shall we let wife and
daughters work in household matters, under the
warm shelter of their own roof; shall we let them
cook, sew, and make beds with a limited amount
of assistance, and put by money for the future ; or
shall we carefully avoid even every appearance of
their doing so, and spend all our income ?" The
wife is generally the first to say, " My dear, we
must keep up the children's *position ; "* and, poor
woman, there is some excuse for her, since her
neighbour appears to impose such terms. Deep
into the heart of English society eats this cankering
notion that women of the middle class lose caste
by household activity. It is a notion rather than a
reality, as those who attempt to brave it soon dis-
cover. But there it is, enthroned in endless rows
and terraces, and crescents and squares,—where-

ever the poor but genteel merchant, and the second-
rate professional men reside ; men with from £300
to £400 per annum, and a growing-up family ; men
who *might* save a little, men who *might* insure, but
who keep two servants and do neither. If, indeed,
the girls had been withdrawn from household work,
in order that they might be fitted for some remunerative employment, there would be no cause of
complaint ; but, in the first place, there *never will*
be remunerative employment for the majority of
middle-class women. They are meant to marry,
and would marry much oftener, even in the present
state of overflow of numbers, were there a little
portion ready for the marriage-day. But there is
neither portion nor legacy. There comes a day of
weeping and mourning, a day when the master lies
cold and still in his upstairs room ; when the hearse
carries him away, and the mother assumes her
widow's cap. Then the two servants have to be
dismissed. Then the young brothers seek for
situations as best they may, and the daughters likewise. But the youths succeed, and the girls fail.
For a while they keep together, but that must end.
The young man emigrates, marries, perhaps death

takes him also ; and the mother and daughters are
helped on by friends, exhaust their little store of
well-wishers, take in sewing, drift lower and lower
out into that vast ocean of destitution, of which the
shores are so steep that a bold swimmer and a hard
climber may hardly ascend the brink thereof.

IV.

THE PROFESSION OF THE
TEACHER.

THE PROFESSION OF THE TEACHER.*

N casting a preliminary glance over the vast field of female paid labour in this country, a field which may be roughly calculated to embrace about three millions of women, or half its female population, I am well assured that one department will chiefly interest the majority of my readers—namely, the Profession of the Teacher. And this for an obvious reason, that it was until lately almost the only profession open to an educated woman of average ability. Few realise the extent to which women of the lower classes are employed in undomestic labour, in the factory, the workship, and the field; —but while *all* my lady readers have received instruction from some class of governess, there is

* The Annual Reports of the Governesses' Benevolent Institution, from 1843 to 1864.

probably not one who has not also some relative
or cherished friend either actually engaged in
teaching, or had formerly been so engaged. We
find families who have no link with the army,
the navy, or the church ; others, who in all their
wide-spread connexion have kept aloof from trade ;
—but from the highest to the lowest rank in which
a liberal education is bestowed, we shall find some
cousin or friend who is a governess. Indeed, it is
not a question of rank at all, for the unmarried
female members of the small merchant's family
enter the profession from natural necessity, and
the fortuneless daughters of the highly connected
clergyman have often no other resource. It is a
platform on which middle and upper classes meet,—
the one struggling up, the other drifting down. If
a father dies, or a bank breaks, or a husband is
killed,—if brothers require a college education to
fit them for one of the many careers open to an
M.A., or orphan nephews and nieces are cast helpless upon a woman's heart, here is the one means
of breadwinning to which access alone seems open
—to which alone untrained capacity is equal, or
pride admits appeal.

This brief statement sums up the conclusion to which many melancholy narratives of dire suffering and long struggle furnish ample evidence ; and there is perhaps no social reform for which the time is so ripe, or which English men and women would so eagerly carry out, as any reasonable plan for getting rid of this particular form of destitution, arising in great measure from the overcrowding of the Profession of the Teacher. To the attainment of this end two distinct modes of action are available, with a heavy penalty on the neglect of *either*. We must relieve existing needs, and, if possible, prevent their recurrence ;—the one course demands the best sympathies of the heart, the other the best exertions of the intellect.

Towards the first object, that of meeting facts as they are, a vast effort has been made during the course of the last twenty years. The story is told in the series of reports which we have placed as a note to the heading of this chapter, and it is evident that in rallying, so to speak, the members of the profession round this group of institutions, an indirect effect to the great advantage of its general status has also been produced, and a cer-

tain *esprit de corps* infused, which has a strong
tendency to raise the rate of attainment and the
rate of salary. We will condense the leading facts
of this narration, which places in the strongest,
the most startling light, the extent of that suffering
which the institution was designed to relieve; and
shows, no less remarkably, the power of a few
kind hearts and clear heads, when also backed up
by unflinching wills for twenty years.

The germ of the institution dates from the year
1841, but little was done until 1843, when the
society was newly organised, many members were
added to the committee, and the Rev. David
Laing undertook the office of honorary secretary.
On application to the late Duke of Cambridge,
he presided at a public meeting in the month of
May of the latter year; the Duchess of Gloucester,
the Duchess of Cambridge, and the Queen Dow-
ager gave their names; subscriptions were entered
and donations bestowed; and within a month of
the public meeting the first practical plan was
organised for action, in the form of a ladies' committee, for "affording assistance privately and
delicately to ladies in temporary distress." The

committee met once a fortnight, and the amount
of actual *destitution* among educated women, which
thus came to their ears, is appalling to imagine.
Many who would have shrunk from appealing to
private charity "hailed the establishment of the
institution as a message from Providence to save
them from despair;" and from the month of June
1843 until the following March, the ladies' committee received and examined a hundred and two
cases, and assisted fifty-six; of the remainder the
greater number were "reluctantly declined for
want of sufficient funds." The report gives a sad
classification of some of the cases relieved in this
first year's work ; one woman had "saved nothing
during twenty-six years of exertion, having supported her mother, three younger sisters, and a
brother, and educated the four." Three were
entirely empoverished by attempts to uphold their
fathers' efforts in business. Six were burdened
by the support of invalid sisters who had no other
props in life; and three were *incapable of taking
another situation from extreme nervous excitement,
caused by over exertion and anxiety*. In short, says
the report, "the inquiries made into these cases

may be briefly stated to show how many governesses spend the early part of their lives *in working for others."* Her time of exertion comprising
" twenty-five years at the utmost, at a salary com-
mencing at £25, and seldom exceeding £80 per
annum, if domestic ties take part of her savings,
or if ill health come, attended by that worst of all
pains, *compulsory rest*—not only stopping the ac-
cumulation of her little fund, but instantly preying
on it—how shall the governess provide for herself
in her old age ? "

As some slight solution of this fearful question—
fearful when the sex, the years, and the probable
physical delicacy of the class referred to are considered—the general committee set themselves to
work to found annuities for aged governesses. In
this first year £500 was got together, and invested
to create a perpetual annuity of £15 ; and for this
small yearly sum there at once appeared about
thirty candidates, *many of them entirely destitute.*

By 1850 the number of annuitants at £15 per
annum was seventeen, for which annuities a proportionate capital had been raised, while twenty-
five received £20, and one annuity amounted to

£30. These annuities were all *permanent*, and upon the death of any recipient another is elected.

In like manner, 1852 saw the ladies' committee distributing temporary assistance to the amount of £1000 a year.

The third branch of exertion consisted in the formation of provident annuities, paid for by the teachers themselves. Contracts were made at the National Debt office, on better terms than the Life Assurance offices would afford; and between March 1843 and March 1844 the honorary secretary received £2351, 9s. 9d. from ladies towards the purchase of annuities for themselves. In 1856 the amount received was £8758; and two hundred and seventy-four ladies had *secured* their annuities, "an amount of permanent usefulness to the society's credit, which is often overlooked by those of its friends who think more of the relief of distress than of its prevention." The *total* amount received for provident annuities during the working of this branch had reached in 1864 to the enormous sum of £147,600.

The general principle of assurance is so little applied or understood by the female sex, that no greater kindness can be done to working women than to put them in the way of such safe and profitable investments of their earnings, thus helping them to modes of self-help which they have neither the knowledge nor the courage to attempt alone.

In 1844 another branch of usefulness was planned, namely, a temporary home for governesses out of situations, where they could be more cheaply and respectably lodged than elsewhere; and in connexion with this home, a system of free registration. The latter plan was first carried into operation at the office in 1845, and in 1846 was transferred to the home, which received, during the first six months of its existence, fifty-two governesses as inmates.

Finally, in 1849, an aged asylum was completed and inhabited, and in 1856 its inmates numbered twenty-two.

Our readers will perhaps be tired of all these dates and figures, but only by their aid can we present even the slightest outline of what has been done by this long series of labours. We will now gladly turn to some of the many beautiful anecdotes of tender Christian feeling among these numbers

of women, both among those who gave and those
who received ; nay, in some cases, the poorest were
also the givers.   We find in one of the earliest reports that, particulars having reached the ladies'
committee of a young governess who was dying at
Cheltenham, a request was forwarded to a friend
in that distant town, who adopted the duty of the
metropolitan institution, and watched her to the
last.   In May, of the same year, a lady sent £15
to be divided among the unsuccessful candidates
for annuities ; another sent £7 for the same purpose ; and in November "an anonymous friend
sent through Messrs Hoare the noble donation of
£100, to be divided amongst ten of the unsuccessful candidates at the discretion of the committee."
This friend afterwards proved to be Dr Thackeray,
Provost of King's College, Cambridge, who, on
his decease in 1851, bequeathed an annuity to the
society.

Here is a short story of a more delicate and
tender kindness than humanity can often claim
to record.   The following letter was received from
a former successful annuitant, whose *whole income was* £40 :—

" I am quite happy here, and rather useful to
my fellow-creatures. I purposed writing next
month to Mr Laing, to do me a very great favour
next polling-day.

" I want him to be so good as to take the
trouble to select from the poorest, the most friend-
less, the shabbiest dressed of my sister governesses,
who may the next-polling-day present themselves,
and necessarily retire disappointed ; ask him to in-
vite such an one to spend a month with me. I
shall give the heartiest welcome, and try to warm
and cheer her the December time, whoever she
may be, agreeable or the reverse. I shall try to
live nicely during her sojourn. The mercies I at
this moment enjoy ought for a few weeks to be
shared with the disappointed ! " Meeting this in-
vitation as it deserved, a lady was sent to whom
change of air and kindness were deemed most
valuable, and the visitor remained "nine weeks
under her peaceful roof," remarking of her hostess,
in a letter, " Often have I seen her, aged as she is,
making up, in a suitable way, garments for the
poor, that she had begged for the purpose from her
richer neighbours. It is astonishing to see how

much she contrives to do for her fellow-creatures,
with an amount per annum that would by many be
deemed too small to procure bread and cheese for
herself."

With regard to the great age which occasionally
marks the candidates, we find that, in 1851, Miss
Maurice, an unwearied friend to the institution,
collected enough money to entitle herself to a pre-
sentation to the asylum, which was given to an
aged lady, eighty-one years old; a period of human
existence at which it is somewhat painful not to
know "where to lay one's head."

The eighth annuity founded (in 1845) was at the
suggestion of the Bishop of Durham, who offered
to give £50, if nine other parties would contribute
the same amount, towards the necessary £500.
Six other names were received in a fortnight.

One more extract and we have done. It is a sort
of cornice to all the preceding ones. The report for
1857 states that " on a recent occasion there were
one hundred and twenty candidates for three annuities of £20 each. One hundred and twenty ladies,
many reared in affluence, and all accustomed to the
comforts and luxuries of at least our middle ranks—

G

all seeking an annuity of £20! Of these ninety-nine were unmarried; and out of this number four-teen had incomes of, or above, £20, eleven derived from public institutions or private benevolence, and three from their own savings; twenty-three had incomes varying from TWENTY SHILLINGS to £17; and eighty-three had absolutely NOTHING. It will be recollected that all these ladies are above fifty years of age; and, of the utterly destitute, forty-nine were above sixty."

Here we close our account of one of the most remarkable charities of modern times, which is at this moment pursuing its active career, and which, in drawing attention to an amount of sheer desti-tution before unsuspected, will create final results far more extensive than the immediate relief to in-dividuals. Yet we may well ask ourselves what would have become of these individuals, but for such timely relief? The more aged recipients of annuities or inmates of the asylum would have lived with relatives, not with children, for a small proportion are married; and in innumerable in-stances they must have depended on the slender earnings of nieces whom they had brought up to their own profession, thus laying the seed for fresh misery of a like kind. A glance over the many cases wherein teachers have been the only supports of orphans will confirm the truth of this assertion ; for when their own " aged mother " and " invalid sisters " are dead, on whom can they lean in life except upon the children whom they have fed and taught upon their own insufficient means? When even this refuge fails them, they literally come upon the *workhouse*. Nor is this, O tender-hearted reader, an imagination. Go thou into our parish workhouses in dreary London, and investigate the past histories of some of those pale figures lying on the narrow couches of the female wards, and thou wilt find there drifted waifs and strays from the "upper and middle classes" who pass long months and years in pauper clothing upon a pauper's fare.

Such a search would convince the brave and honest independence of those who say, " Let us work hard while we have strength, on the terms that society allows ; and when we cannot do so any more, let us suffer privation in silence, let us not accept charity as a substitute for sufficient wages," that the wide-spread efforts made for governesses during the last fifteen years have been justified by the occasion. No one who accepts the Christian religion as a rule of life can deny what Turks and Pagans both preach and practise, --that the simple direct effort to relieve pain and poverty is one of the primary duties of a human creature. In a highly "civilised" community, where a degraded class exists who live systematically upon the fruits of begging, and whom indiscriminate aid can only corrupt further, there may be cogent reasons against street-giving of halfpence to blind beggars with baskets, and destitute families with six small children of impossible relative ages, walking in a graduated procession at a snail's trot. But while listening to the political economist, who warns us that charity is often only another name for self-indulgence in feeling, sowing the seeds of greater misery than it professes to alleviate, we must not forget that the limitations to this doctrine imposed by justice and by religion are sufficient of themselves to constitute a positive code. We must *not* train up any class to depend on the exertions of others; but we *must* set ourselves to work to

help those who suffer, in such a way as may tend
to lessen their present pain and their future need,
without counting too closely the money value of
the precious ointment bestowed upon that humanity which we share in common.

It is much to be doubted whether the action of our
poor law, doling out scanty help with a grudging
hand, which seems to offer an ill-defined right in
the place of honest charity, is not more degrading
to our lower classes than almsgiving. Assuredly
it is more degrading than alms bestowed by those
who throw their hearts in with them. But at any
rate it is our plainest duty to feed the hungry and to
clothe the naked, and to afford shelter to the aged,
while striving that benefit to the individual shall
not result in injury and degradation to the class.

For, be it observed, life is no such smooth and
easy matter that we can say of any one who has
fallen into misfortune that it is his or her fault, or that
of any one now living. It has pleased Providence
to place us in a moral atmosphere of so many
mingled elements that we cannot in many cases
assign the particular causes of a particular poverty.
There are such things as hereditary diseases and

hereditary incapacity; — banks will break, and
swallow up the fortunes of helpless hundreds, and
a commercial crisis drags into its vortex houses
which were guiltless of speculation or expense.
And so we see on all hands, that, while certain
general laws can be discovered which form the
moral scheme of Providence, there come up indivi
dual questions every day which cannot be settled
by reference to any such laws. We know, as a
matter of certainty, that the drunken workman
will bring his children to hunger and cold ;—yet
we cannot, therefore, let the children die. We
may come to fixed conclusions as to the causes
which lie at the root of the difficulty of earning a
livelihood experienced by ladies ; yet we none the
less have *this* generation of such ladies to care for,
remembering the story of the good Samaritan, who,
when he saw that the stranger was wounded, did
not stop to speculate on the best way of rendering
roads secure from thieves, but *went to him and
bound up his wounds.*

I have entered on this dry explanation of what
I conceive to be the right way of viewing large
public charities privately administered, because I

believe there are many people of intellect and conscience, alike among the rich and the poor, who recoil from the idea of giving or of receiving any material aid. I believe, with the whole might of my convictions, that for human creatures to help one another freely, when that love which is the bread of life is given together with the bread that perisheth, honours both the giver and the receiver, and can be degrading to none.   I have every reason to believe that, in this particular instance of the Governesses' Benevolent Institution, the greatest, the most sisterly tenderness and delicacy has been shown in the transactions between the society (as represented by its lady members) and the teachers, while the remarkable results obtained by the funds placed at their disposal show the zealous attention which must have been bestowed upon the institution by experienced men ; and the mass of *facts* thus brought to light serve as a safe and sufficient basis of argument for those more diffusive efforts which will tend to cut off the evil at its source, by directing the industry of educated women into other and more profitable channels.

Let us now turn to this, after all, most important side of the question, and see upon what point of certainty we can first fix our attention. It is the opinion of the gentleman who has for years acted as honorary secretary, (a post which has in this instance been anything but a mere name,) and under whose observation all the accumulated details of the various connected institutions have fallen—it is his decided opinion that the number of *first-class* governesses is not greater than the demand for their services, and that, although, taking this for granted, the salary of a woman of unusual professional ability and attainment cannot rise higher than that of a small government clerk, at from £100 to £200 a year, still this sum can be secured, and absolute penury avoided. But this supposes the governess to be highly accomplished according to the standard now insisted upon by the "nobility and gentry," to be well conversant with two or more foreign languages, and to be marked in dress and manner by all the elegance of a highly-bred lady. Such a woman, capable of teaching Horace to little Lord Edward, and of reading Dante and Schiller with young Lady Isa

bella, will probably secure what is considered to
be relatively, if not absolutely, a "good salary."
Where, then, falls the strain? The question is
easily answered; it falls upon the hundreds and
thousands of women who, born in the middle-class,
live by its instruction; upon the daughters of professional men, who, educated themselves in the
conventional degree of knowledge and accomplishments, suddenly, at the death of a parent, or the
failure of an investment, rush into the profession
of the teacher, and discharge its duties in all probability with honesty and thoroughness so far as
they are able, but without any of that nicety of ac-
quirement, or peculiar tact and science in imparting, which would enable them to outbid the hosts
of sister governesses who are teaching on the same
social level, and for equally low pay. The over-
supply of teachers has, moreover, reacted on the
custom of the employers, who have set their ideas
to a certain scale, and, if they educate their children at home, refuse to pay beyond a certain percentage on the whole family income for their instruction.

It remains for us to see what can be done to

kill this evil at its root. How much can be done to mitigate its consequences may be read in these reports; but, after all, the *greatest* benefit achieved by the group of institutions of which they treat, consists in the degree of attention which they have drawn to the state of the profession at large. One part of the question is already in course of being answered. Every year sees an ever-increasing number of women devoting themselves to the fine arts. Their names are scattered about in the catalogue of the Royal Academy, and a special exhibition has existed for nine years for the reception of works by female artists. Literature again is followed, as a profession, by women, to an extent far greater than our readers are at all aware of. The magazines of the day are filled by them; one of the oldest and best of our weekly periodicals owes two-thirds of its contents to their pens. Even the leaders of our newspapers are, in some instances, regularly written by women, and publishers avail themselves largely of their industry in all manner of translations and compilations. In the reading-room of the British Museum, that magnificent abode of learning, the roving eye may any day detect the bowed heads and black silk dresses of ladies who come there for references on every subject under heaven; searching out obscure hints concerning ways and words of defunct princesses, or well-nigh forgotten manipulations of mediæval trades.

But the number of women who are adopting pursuits connected with literature and the arts must not blind us to the fact that they will always constitute the minority among even " skilled labourers." For the smallest aptitude with the pen, and what would appear to be a very average power of arranging ideas in sequence, is not a very widely diffused intellectual gift. Among men, how small is the *comparative* number of artists and authors !—the hacks may perhaps be reckoned by thousands, the average writers by hundreds, the geniuses by tens. But when we speak of unemployed women, it is a question of *tens of thousands*. What, then, will the arts do for them, when every other woman one meets is ready to assure one that she could not write for the press " to save her life ?"

About seven years ago, when this subject was

first acquiring prominence, and when less sympathy
for the struggles of unemployed women was felt
than now exists, much ridicule was cast (I believe
in the *Saturday Review*) upon a sentence in Madame Bodichon's little pamphlet, entitled *Women
and Work.* The sentence, which was quoted as
the *ne plus ultra* of wild arithmetic, runs thus—it
occurs at the close of some remarks on female
destitution :—

"Apprentice 10,000 to watchmakers; train 10,000
for teachers for the young; make 10,000 good accountants; put 10,000 more to be nurses under
deaconesses trained by Florence Nightingale; put
some thousands in the electric telegraph offices all
over the country; educate 1000 lecturers for mechanics' institutions; 1000 readers to read the best
books to the working people; train up 10,000 to
manage washing-machines, sewing-machines, &c.
Then the distressed needlewomen would vanish;
the decayed gentlewomen and broken-down governesses would no longer exist."

Now, to isolate this sentence so as to make it
appear that any one person, or any dozen of committees, is expected thus to parcel out the popula-

tion by thousands, is an absurdity which we are
very sure was never contemplated by the writer of
this energetic little pamphlet. It is merely a rapid
summing up of the scale on which relief must be
afforded before the enormous classes of destitute
women, from the refined lady to the

> " Eighty thousand women in one smile,
>   Who only smile at night beneath the gas,"

can be raised to the point of prosperous industry.

If, as may be seen in examining the census,
forty-three per cent. of women above the age of
twenty are either unmarried or widowed ;—if one
half of the female population of the country are
paid labourers ;—if, as the reports adverted to in
this chapter suppose, the number of governesses
alone may be assumed at fifteen thousand, and the
number of paupers and worse than paupers enor-
mously larger,—then it is evident that an ideal
distribution of the gross amount into other employ-
ments by tens of thousands is merely a forecasting
of the results which we must set ourselves to obtain
somehow.

OTHER PROFESSIONS.

OTHER PROFESSIONS.

HEN moral and material causes combine to effect changes in the same
direction, it is not always easy to
divide the responsibility between them. The great
extent of female destitution is chiefly due to economical changes and shortcomings, and can only
be dealt with by economical reforms; but the
great increase of female activity in this generation
is chiefly due to other circumstances. Women
would neither starve, nor, except in very limited
numbers, become teachers if they could help it;
but they would in numerous cases silently follow
other and more intellectual avocations, and are
constantly found to do so with great delight and
profit where no pecuniary need exists. To make
any practical distinction between the two orders of
working women would be impossible; they run

into each, and are confounded at every turn in the *higher* walks of industry. Many a woman who was forced to work has found that genius developed under the happy necessity; and such are no subjects of pity, but should rather bless the privation of worldly riches which set them free.

Not only have we a large number of single women working successfully in literary and artistic pursuits, but very many married women also, who, so far from neglecting their families, have helped to provide for them, or if widowed, have wholly provided for them by their exertions; and they have been enabled to do this partly because the scientific improvements of the time have allowed the physical necessities of domestic life to be supplied with far less personal trouble than formerly.

It is become a stock phrase that the household customs of our grandmothers are fast wearing away in every class of society. In the upper ranks they have become "fine by degrees and beautifully less," till their trace is almost imperceptible. Among the middle ranks, the introduction of the sewing machine will gradually banish the chief domestic industry which yet remains. In a few

years the making of shirts and dresses by hand will
become as much a tradition amongst us as is now
the use of the spinning-wheel ; and though any lady
who believes that a piece of silk dropped in at one
end is turned out a complete garment at the other,
(deftly fashioned like a Birmingham pin,) is under
a delusion as to the exact nature of this wonderful
invention, still the headwork required to direct its
operation is but small, and an alarming amount of
human ingenuity is set free.

In cookery the same substitution of mechanical
aids is also taking place—small households find
the toil lightened, and steam ranges, and all
the other paraphernalia of a first-class kitchen,
cause a great diminution of labour to the *chef;*
and should the continental fashion of eating
in common increase in this country, the application of such contrivances on a large scale
will become generally possible. Water now
conveyed by pipes to the top of every well-built
house, "lifts" transferred from the warehouse to
the club, and from thence to the private dwelling,
gas stoves, or gas *fires*, like the beautiful and
cleanly specimen exhibited in the Crystal Palace,

all tend to diminish the amount of the household labour of women. The inventive tendencies of the present time have lately set strongly in this direction, and we have at least learnt not to be sceptical on the score of the possibilities of science. Who knows that our houses may not shortly become " self-acting," may not wash their own steps, scrub their own floors, light their own fires, and be generally capable of turning themselves " out of windows?" On this point Theodore Parker has said eloquent words. In a discourse delivered by him at Boston, in 1858, entitled " The Public Function of Woman," occurs this passage on partially unoccupied women :—

"In the progress of mankind, and the application of masculine science to what was once only feminine work,—whereby so much time is saved from the wheel and the loom, the oven and the spit, with the consequent increase of riches, the saving of time, and the intellectual education which comes in consequence thereof,—this class of women is continually enlarging. With us in New England, in all the north, it is a very large class. . . . . . It is a great deal larger than most men commonly think it is. It is continually enlarging, and you see why. When all manufactures were domestic,— when every garment was made at home, every web wove at home, every thread spun at home, every fleece dyed at home, —when the husband provided the wool or the sheepskin, and the wife made it a coat,—when the husband brought home a sack of corn on a mule's back, and the wife pounded it in a mortar, or ground it between two stones, as in the Old Testament,—then the domestic function might well consume all the time of a very able-headed woman. But now-a-days, when so much work is done abroad,—when the flour-mills of Rochester and Boston take the place of the pestle and mortar, and the hand-mill of the Old Testament,—when Lowell and Lawrence are two enormous Old Testament women, spinning and weaving year out and year in, day and night both,—when so much of woman's work is done by the butcher and the baker, by the tailor and the cook and the gas-maker, and she is no longer obliged to dip or mould with her own hands every candle that goeth not out by night,' as in the Old Testament woman's house-keeping,—you see how very much of woman's time is left for other functions. This will become yet more the case. Ere long, a great deal of lofty science will be applied to housekeeping, and work be done by other than human hands in the house, as out of it. And, accordingly, you see that the class of women not wholly taken up by the domestic function will get larger and larger."

The experience of New England and that of Old England is alike, and creates a corresponding tendency among our young women to enter upon professional life ; some on the spur of a stern necessity, others inspired by a hearty enthusiasm, others making a compromise between the two modes of life, and gasping a perpetual protestation of womanhood, while stitching together the old cloth and the new.

One profession after another responds to the pressure from without, and opens its enclosure to the gentle demand. Sometimes the gates are slowly forced back with an almost imperceptible movement, at other times suddenly unclose, as when a Florence Nightingale or a Rosa Bonheur gives to society the result of long hidden labours, to posterity the echo of a hitherto unknown name.

In the last century it was a hard matter for a woman even to write. Miss Carter, the Greek scholar and translator of Epictetus, was currently reported to be about to be returned as "member for Deal." Poems which we should now consider as unworthy an Oxford prize, gained quite a reputation for their fair writers in the social circle, and the professional authoress enjoyed a certain horrible eminence, such as we assign in our imagination to a man who walks upon stilts.

A few lettered ladies of rank and refinement made glad the hearts of authors and of artists in the drawing-rooms of Leicester and Bloomsbury

Squares. Very few women wrote for bread, and
the tone of literature, as regarded the sex, was of
the worst description. Mrs Macaulay, one of the
limited sisterhood of the pen, amiably alludes to
"those vices and foibles which are peculiar to the
female sex; vices and foibles which have caused
them to be considered in ancient times as beneath
cultivation, and *in modern days have subjected them
to the censure and ridicule of writers of all descrip-
tions.*" Whoso remembers the allusions to women
in the *Tatler*, the *Spectator*, and even in the *Ram-
bler*, will acknowledge the truth of the assertion
which we have italicised. It was time that women
should take up the pen, if only to purify the young
periodical press which delighted in such a topic of
abuse. It one day happened to me at "gooseberry
time," to be drinking tea in an old farm house.
Piled up on a shelf above the door, a shelf inac-
cessible even to a farmer six feet high, were a
dozen old volumes, bound in thick brown binding.
By the help of a chair, the dusty treasures were
brought down; they proved to be *Lady's Magazines* for 1790, and succeeding years,—their contents indescribable to modern ears. Such feeble

poems, such ineffable stories, such disgracefully
scandalous anecdotes of people in high life, with
all the vowels omitted from their names, and occasionally portraits of a disreputable hero or heroine,
types from Newgate or Doctors' Commons. Such
was the nascent literature which has been replaced
by *Chambers's Journal* and *Household Words*,—such
the arena upon which women were about to enter
in numbers, helping to create what we popularly
call " the Press."

With the growth of the press has grown the
direct influence of educated women on the world's
affairs. Mute in the senate and in the church,
their opinions have found a voice in sheets of
ten thousand readers. First in the list of their
achievements came admirable novels, not because
fiction can be written without knowledge, but because it only requires that knowledge which they
can most easily attain,—the result of insight into
humanity. As periodicals have waxed numerous,
so has female authorship waxed strong. The
magazines demanded short graphic papers, observation, wit, and moderate learning,—women demanded work such as they could perform at home,

and ready pay upon performance; the two wants
met, and the female sex has become a very important element in the fourth estate. If editors
were ever known to disclose the dread secrets of
their dens, they only could give the public an idea
of the authoresses whose unsigned names are
Legion; of their rolls of manuscripts, which are as
the sands of the sea.

Since this direct influence of women, exerted in
periodical literature, now extends from the quarterly to the monthly, from the monthly to the
weekly and daily press, embracing all topics, from
the weightiest to the lightest, politics, morals, art,
literature, and the ephemera of the day; since it is
backed up by a serious cultivation, among an increasing minority, of those branches of knowledge
which require volumes for their elucidation, and
a lifetime for their due research, we may fairly
regard the literary profession as one already conquered by its feminine aspirants. We have placed
it at the beginning of our list, because it is in one
sense the easiest of all. Its successful exercise
demands little or none of that moral courage which
more public avocations require. It shows, how-

ever, to a most remarkable extent, what a latent
vigour there is in the intellect of women, ready to
flow forth into any channels, could these be easily
cut.

The next profession which we will take into consideration is that of the artist. The female artist
is, in England, also the creation of the century.
One swallow does not make a summer, and
Angelica Kauffmann, gaining access to the Academy, was the fortunate accident of her day,
nor can she be fairly regarded as having risen
above mediocrity in her painting. Her beauty,
her accomplishments, her virtues and her mis-
fortunes, gained for her a fame to which her
professional excellence alone could scarcely have
entitled her. But the same rising current which
bore so many women into literature has of late
years divided, and part of the stream sets steadily
for the realms of art. This is exemplified not
only by the progressive achievements, but even
by the very failures of female artists. Not only
young women of special talent, but young women
possessing very little, now devote themselves to
one of the many branches which cover the whole

debateable land between the sublime and the ridiculous. Some of these, such as wood-engraving, require only perseverance and delicacy, and if a girl has to earn her livelihood, and is clever and ambitious, she thinks twice as to whether she will try writing in the magazines or attending the classes at Kensington, and a trifling weight decides the scale.

But it is infinitely more difficult to draw passably well than to write passably well, and for this simple reason, that our ordinary education furnishes us with the main instruments of literature, while the *méchanique* of art is a study unconnected with any other. Grammar and composition are taught to every child at school, they are involved in most other lessons, it being usual to require written abstracts in history and philosophy, and of every subject capable of being so treated ; but perspective and colour claim in a school-girl's education but scanty time and care.

The art-student has, therefore, to acquire a whole technical language of lines and hues, and when these are acquired, she demands space, freedom, quietness, and unbroken hours before they

can be made available; and when they are made
available, there are still the nobler heights of intellect and imagination to be scaled. It is possible to
write fine things at a desk in the corner of the
kitchen; Jean Paul penned his great works while
his mother tormented him to her heart's content;
but it is not possible to paint without a studio, or
some sort of separation from the noise and bustle
of the external world.

Therefore, to become a good artist requires
talent, industry, and opportunity, and added to all
these, a large share of that moral courage which
dares to dedicate a life to one end, and sweeps
aside, with deliberate calmness, the petty temptations, the accumulated distractions of domestic
hours.

Nor are the mere appliances of study yet entirely
under the command of the female student: the
life-class is a difficulty. Yet without it they had
far better resign all idea of painting the figure.
Nor is the practice of landscape art much easier to
a woman, unless she have a very determined will
and very thick boots. Long hours of exposure to
sun and wind are inevitable, and free access to

nature for months at a time ; a large amount of personal freedom ; and a courageous exercise of personal independence. Health would certainly be gained in the pursuit, and feminine beauty need not be sacrificed ; but how persuade the world of this,—the world of opinion which clings so obstinately, (and not without truth,) to the old belief that

" Her face is her fortune."

Truly, among women, the pursuit of even landscape art is certainly " the pursuit of knowledge under difficulties by female examples;" and in consequence, not much has yet been done amongst us. With the heartiest interest, the keenest sympathy in their labour, we cannot but confess we have as yet no women artists who take rank with our writers of even fifty years ago. No pencil as clear, strong, and animated as Maria Edgeworth's pen—no etching delicate and vivid as Jane Austen's style—no palette as amply stored with pure and lovely colour as the pages of Mary Mitford—with the profounder tints of feeling, as the delineations of Mrs Inchbald. Our female painters are too much upon the level of Mrs Hemans or L. E. L.

full of sparkling incorrectness, tender, misty imagination, and ambition that overleaps itself. One
lady paints Italian scenes with the desperate brush
of Mrs Ratcliffe ; another gives us truth and pathos
mixed up with the ugly simplicity of the shepherd
of Salisbury plain ; others shower upon us those
delusive reproductions of some admired master's
style, which are like electrotypes of the real thing
— quite hollow.

To how few names can we look with pride! How
few have attained that recognised position which is
necessary, not for ambition's sake, but because, if
they are to stimulate others, and to clear a new and
beautiful field of labour for women, it can only be
done by that definite achievement of which the
perfect works of the Creator offer us examples per-
petually. God's works are complete in themselves,
and immeasurably suggestive beyond the line of
their completion. Something of this completeness
must be attained in works of art, before the higher
and more mystical meanings evolve. In vaster
forms—as in mountain ranges—in the plays of
Shakespeare, the frescoes of Michael Angelo, we
may allow for ideas roughly indicated and bound-

aries undefined. But in lesser things a want of perfectness is a want of truth.

In another profession, that of the sculptor, we have very few labourers. Everything we have said of painters will also apply to students of the plastic art; but it is even more difficult of attainment by women; its materials more cumbrous, its opportunities more rare. Harriet Hosmer, Susan Durant, Mrs Thorneycroft, Felicie de Fauvean, and Rosa Bonheur (who occasionally models exquisite groups,) are the only names which occur to the memory.

We now come to the one art in which women have, from first to last, achieved success, renown, and emolument commensurate with those of its male professors,—the histrionic art. Who will award the palm between Garrick and Mrs Siddons? To what actor shall we assign pre-eminence over Rachel and Ristori? The queens of the drama have swayed the world, and won for themselves the brightest honours. And why? Because in their profession natural endowment is almost everything, while the *curriculum*, though necessary, is of comparatively small importance; because, moreover, they were absolutely necessary to the development

of the art, and have therefore been aided, encour-
aged, and protected in its exercise by the other
sex. Everything has been done to *prevent* women
excelling in other departments, not out of *malice
prepense,* but according to a preconceived theory as
to their proper sphere; they have been debarred
from all those institutions where young men fit
themselves for active life; and their deeds have
been small as their opportunities. But for the
training of the actress nothing is omitted. The
fine voice and the stately step, the intellectual dis-
crimination and the enthusiastic mood,—all are
taken advantage of, and carried to their utmost
perfection. Honour and riches await success; and
to the free exercise of all the faculties in this profession we owe some of the noblest—we are thank-
ful also to add, some of the *best*—women the world
has seen. But we must not consider only the
eminent stars. Let my readers also remember to
how large a number of female subordinates the
stage also gives employment, in all its branches; to
how many ranges of talent and of character; to
how many walking voices, and standing lay figures;
to how many dancing feet; to how much of trial

and temptation,—to how much also of virtue and heroism it affords scope.

It is a world within a world, and one too little regarded in discussions as to the practical possibility of organising female labour to a lucrative point. If spoken of at all, it is rather to "point a moral, or adorn a tale," and to be held up as an example of mischief. Yet I feel sure that this is a very unfair generalisation ; there is a great deal to be said about the theatrical profession which never has been said yet, and which can only be said by one intimately acquainted with its details. The incomes gained by its various classes of members, and their average distribution ; the effect of their occupation on the relations of domestic life ; and many other points of the deepest and most practical interest, require a wise and sincere treatment, which I trust they will one day obtain from a competent pen.

There is one career in which many more women might be lucratively engaged ; that of the lecturer or reader, which has for some years been dignified by the unceasing exertions of a few. If women are allowed by public taste to give dra-

matic readings, (and all the civilised world which
can understand English flocks to hear Mrs Fanny
Kemble,) there is no sort of reason to be alleged
why the inferior degrees of theatrical talent, or
impressive elocution, should not be employed with
advantage in the service of Mechanics' Institutes,
and kindred societies. If women can write books
which the world will gladly read, they can also
deliver lectures which the world will gladly hear,
and they may be trusted to do so with ample delicacy and dignity. If Mrs Stowe, when in England,
had given "readings" from Uncle Tom, the
Crystal Palace would not have contained her
audience, and if she might have read her own
novel, why might she not have told the English
people some of the experiences of the "abolition
movement?" Many a woman to whom the earning
of an honest livelihood is an absolute necessity,
would know how to read an interesting paper to
the audiences of our provincial towns, without
departing one iota from the refined demeanour of
private life.

It may be that as time goes on, other professions
and modifications of those now practised will rise

into importance; that of the teacher will surely
receive more attention, and be rendered more
noble in its requirements and in its results. There
yet remain for us to consider the chief obstacles
which meet a woman desirous of adopting any professional career, and the best way of helping her to
overcome them.

The first question raised is invariably this—how
far domestic duties ought to interfere with the
devotion of young women to an art. Of course
where poverty compels recourse to non-domestic
exertion, this question is never raised; but if the
aspirant is in easy circumstances, what then are
the claims of parents, brothers, and sisters, as
opposed to those made by the successful cultivation of a profession? Feeling sure that no law
can be laid down to meet cases which are infinitely
various, and claims which depend on the health,
the age, and even the temperaments of a domestic
circle, I am inclined to urge strongly a few of
those arguments *for* professional life, which may
serve to counterbalance those which many in
authority will be ready to urge against it.

In the first place, the demand made upon a

daughter's time depends very much not only on
the circumstances, but on the rank of the family.
We do not consider respectable labourers or small
shopkeepers to be in a state of poverty, yet the
custom of their class necessitates that its unmarried
female members should work, instead of eating the
bread of idleness at home ; and when from the first
a girl is destined to be apprenticed to a dressmaker, or enter on household service, we hear
nothing of the dreadful gap occasioned by her
absence from the parlour or the kitchen.   It is
accepted as a matter of course, and the parents
console themselves with each other and with the
younger children, while the occasional return of
the stranger is a far greater pleasure than her
absence is a pain.   The way in which the female
members of a family of middle station live together
after they have attained mature years, causes a
grievous waste of moral and mental power.   Four or
five ladies inhabiting one sitting room are too often
like the famous cats of Kilkenny ; they mutually
devour each other's time, leaving nothing but " the
tails " or remnants of useful hours.   The aristocracy manage better, they have more rooms, and

habits of greater separation. It is our middle
class which continues to lay aside the necessities
of the one, the refinements of the other rank, en-
tailing on itself an amount of household inconve-
nience, which is too often only matched by the
amount of household ill-temper.

Days thus frittered away lose all the charm
of periodical activity, of that wondrous play of
action and reaction in which the animate creation exists and delights. Goethe said that the
happiest man was he who best understood how
to secure the regular recurrence of the greatest
number of simple pleasures,—to whom dawn
and twilight, rest and rising, food and fasting,
winter and summer brought perpetual change of
enjoyment which the mind could at once remember
and anticipate. The pulses of nature beat with a
beautiful regularity, and the spiritual tides of man's
being ebb and flow in unison with the tides of the
sea. We are yet the unconscious subjects of
" planetary influence " as truly as was set forth in
the superstitions of the old times; and in regard to
the primal law of order, it is with our frail humanity as with stellar constellations,

"Thou dost preserve the stars from wrong,
And the most ancient heavens through Thee are fresh
and strong."

Now it is in this vital principle of order that the lives of average women are so lamentably deficient. All the power, all the elastic spring which regular intermittent action bestows, is lost in the aimless uncertain current of their hours. It does not matter when they go shopping or when they set out on their calls, and but for the providential and imperious regularity of the digestive organs, they would have but little use for any clock ; and thus are defrauded of one of the chief sources of enjoyment included in the organisation of humanity.

Another objection to the adoption of professional life by women is thus expressed :—" How can fathers be expected to give their daughters expensive special educations, when the probability is that marriage will put a bar to their ever repaying it with success ? " To which we are fain only to ask what happens among the *artistes;* how it is that they continue to combine professional excellence with domestic life ? Let it not be assumed, in reply, that in such cases domestic life is always sacrificed;

many women have fulfilled *both* careers admirably well, and if actresses and singers have conquered the difficulty, in spite of their exciting vocation, surely the painter, the sculptor, might do so likewise.

That the subject is beset with difficulties I do not wish to deny ; but since at the first touch of real necessity we see these difficulties disposed of without any apparent evil result, I believe that the solution for each and all will be found.

VI.

BUSINESS.

BUSINESS.

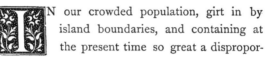N our crowded population, girt in by island boundaries, and containing at the present time so great a disproportion of women, we must expect to find some poverty which no prudence or principle on the part of parents could arrest. That this amount might be greatly lessened is indisputable; nevertheless, we must prepare to deal with what is likely to exist for a long time to come, even if it does not seem (as I confess it does not to my mind) a desirable state of things for great numbers of educated women to be seeking a livelihood out of domestic life.

To what ends, therefore, can we hope to see average women devote themselves, since they cannot sit and starve, and since their natural protectors are gone by thousands across the sea to the antipodes? As a rule, those who can neither write nor

paint, and are not sufficiently educated to teach,
do sink into the grade of mechanical workers, in
which ten shillings a-week is a high average of
wages. But it is very hard that the middle-class
woman, possessing often a fair share of common
knowledge and plenty of sense, should be driven
downwards to such a lot. Could she not in many
more instances join the ranks of *tradeswomen*,
making a tolerable profit, and keeping that which
is so dear to a woman's heart, a comfortable and
respectable roof over her head?

Every race has its *spécialité* of function in the
great aggregation of humanity. While the Hindoo
picks rice, sleeps, bathes, fights, and embroiders
coats of many colours, and the Mohammedan
Arab sits cross-legged in the sun, and plays endless
games of backgammon, the Anglo-Saxon digs and
ploughs, spins and weaves, buys and sells. He is
a sturdy, sensible fellow, has a square forehead
and an active body; he can calculate well, and
usually knows how to buy in the cheapest and sell
in the dearest market. If he be neither literary
nor artistic—and, naturally speaking, he is surely
neither the one nor the other—Mr Bull has a re-

markable share of what is termed "good common sense." Indeed, he prides himself so much upon it, that he will hardly recognise those finer and more spiritual elements which other nations exhibit, and which are as electric forces compared to those of mechanics.

Has his excellent wife no feminine counterpart to his sterling qualities? I think she has. Mrs Bull is what is usually termed a motherly body, and not only looks after the children, but after the store-room too. She weighs the cheese and bacon, and metes out the flannel; she looks after the farmer's men, and flatters her husband's customers with a certain honest frankness delightful to behold. In fine, the Englishwoman in country districts, where many duties lie ready to her hand, and where the mania for rising in life has not turned the best parlour into a boudoir, exemplifies the same type of character as the Englishman. Surely, then, the daughters of our flourishing traders, our small merchants and manufacturers, who remain single for a few, or more than a few years, may find some occupation more healthy, more interesting, and more profitable than that of the inferior gover-

ness.   If such women could more frequently assist
their male relatives as clerks or accountants, or
would enter bravely into any business now open
to their sex, cultivating those virtues of order,
economy, and punctuality which business demands,
they would find themselves far more happily and
successfully engaged, than by rigidly confining themselves to what they deem the gentilities of private
life, and selling themselves to a family of their own
station for £25 a year; and thus the higher class
of governesses, who are fully up to the requirements of the day, would meet with less competition
and more assured pay.

The arts, literature, and tuition might be safely
left to provide for the livelihood of *clever* women,
if *sensible* women would but turn their sense to its
many legitimate spheres of action.   The two great
hindrances, which have frequently met on the
threshold, those who have tried to enforce this
advice in individual cases, have been want of
courage to face social opinion in a new path, and
the want of a little money to start with.

We will take the material hindrance first; and

here again it is to parents, to fathers, that an appeal must be made.

Even if any two young ladies personally known to us were at this moment to be anxious to start in some reputable business, an immediate barrier would probably arise in the want of capital. Girls never have any capital, they hardly know what it means ; yet without it the very first move is impossible ; they may *enter* a shop, but they cannot *own* one.

Consider the great difference between the position of young men and young women in this respect ; the latter have only their pocket-money, sometimes twenty pounds, sometimes thirty pounds a year ; small sums varying according to the means of the middle-class parent, and to the number of his daughters. It is all they can do to dress upon this allowance ; purchase a very few birthday presents, and buy writing-paper and stamps for their limited correspondence. As to being able at any time to command a larger sum, (even this being paid quarterly,) it is a wild and impossible dream ; and it is equally impossible to borrow, as they can

give no security. Many and many a woman lives
to middle age under her parents' roof with no more
money in her purse at one given time than ten
pounds.

But every respectable tradesman manages to
start his son ; it is an item in his life's expenditure
for which he has all along calculated. He knew
he must do it when the boy was born ; and whether he pays to bind him as an apprentice, or helps
him to a share in some business, or supports him
during the first unproductive professional years, it
comes home to him in the shape of money dis-
bursed from his accumulated earnings,—strictly
capital,—or set aside possibly in the latter case
from his own regular income. As a little child, I
used to hear of a certain legend of the last century,
in which a thriving tradesman, finding no vacancy
for his son in his native place, took him on a good
horse, with three hundred pounds of money, to a
fair town thirty miles distant, and there set him up
as a mercer, to the great ultimate success of that
youth. The substantial father, equipped after the
fashion of 1750, trotting along with his boy and his
bag of gold, is a picturesque type of what fathers

do every day, though they go by railway now, and
do not carry their capital in a leather bag. But I
am very much afraid that that tradesman did not
spend three pounds on his daughter; nor, as she
could probably, in those days, bake, and wash, and
brew, and make all her own garments, was her case
a lamentable one as it might be now. Probably
the going out as a governess was the very last
thing that would have entered her head in 1750,
and she either married some comfortable tradesman in her native place, and entered into all his
household necessities, or she lived actively at home,
very little troubled by ideas of gentility and the
deprivations they entail. The arrangements of society answered pretty well for her then; but discre-
pancies have grown up, and they do not answer
now. She will suffer cruelly if she cannot make
a little money to live upon, and she cannot make
money without a little capital to start with : and,
therefore, her chances of marriage being really
diminished, she must work for wages as teacher or
shop-woman, with no hope of setting up on her
own account.

K

It seems, therefore, as if no extensive relief of our suffering class of educated women could be achieved until fathers are won over to see the matter in its true light. But it may be said that fathers cannot afford to give capital, of however small an amount, to their sons and daughters too. But I submit that they are equally bound to their children of either sex, and that in very many cases where they bring their sons up to *professions* and leave their daughters *portionless*, they ought in justice to give the sons a lower and less expensive start in life, and keep some money laid by for their girls.

Moreover, fathers would then gain greatly in the relief of part of their present anxiety, for they certainly love their daughters, and often suffer greatly from fears for their future, though they may not have the courage to break through the social chains which cause those fears. If a girl were taught how to make capital reproductive, instead of merely how to live upon its *interest*, a much less sum would suffice her; and the father who gave or left her a thousand pounds, would bestow upon her a benefit of which he could not calculate the

results, instead of a miserable pittance of thirty
or at most fifty pounds a-year.

In France it is considered morally incumbent
on every parent to settle his daughter in life, and
as a *dot* is an essential part of the matrimonial
contract, every father in a respectable profession or trade considers himself bound to find
a portion for his girl in relative measure to
his position in life. We may complain with
justice that thus to constrain the deepest affections is a great wrong to young Frenchwomen,
and that the wrong doing must bring a host
of moral evils in its train; still we ought to
confess that, according to his light, the French
father does his best for the worldly welfare
of his daughter: he feeds, clothes, and educates.
her in childhood, and when she grows up he set-
tles her in life in that particular line of business
which is considered best, (a line of business which
the *Saturday Review* affirms to be emphatically
her own and her only true career,) and he allots
to her a certain sum as capital, in order that she
may conduct that domestic business of household
economy in the marriage life on terms of mutual

respect and obligation. He does not ask any
man to take her in as "junior partner," on terms
equivalent to board and lodging, and no salary
required ; he does not allow it to be an open question whether her usefulness balances the substantial benefits she receives at his hands. She enters
on equal terms in her woman's capacity, taking
her little fortune and her household management,
just as he takes his money and his work in the
external world to constitute the double fund out
of which they create their well-being. English
readers will shrink from thus regarding marriage as
a commercial firm ; they will say that a husband
and wife are one, and that he must not weigh
what he gives her against what she gives him ;
that such a state of feeling is monstrous, and destructive to all the best and holiest interests of
married life ; and I quite agree with them, I think
that marriage should be wholly independent of
these considerations, that no woman should look
to it as a maintenance. But nobody can deny
that it is very generally considered in that light,
even by the best people ; there is a confusion in
their minds between the Christian theory of the

union of husband and wife, and the political economy which would throw the livelihood of all wives upon the earnings of all husbands. They want to reconcile the two things together, and it is only when they are startled by some very broad assertions, such as that made by the *Saturday Review*, that all women who fail to marry may be considered as having "failed in business," that they are roused up to declare that such a theory of marriage is abominable among a Christian people.

Therefore I would ask all my readers to settle this question quite fairly in their own minds. Is marriage a business relation, or is it not a business relation? or is it, as most people in the depth of their hearts consider it, a judicious mixture of the two? Whichever way you decide, you are on the horns of a dilemma. If it is in ever so small a degree a business, then the French father is quite right to take rigorous care that his daughter be honestly provided with her share of capital, and he is quite right also to try and choose a respectable partner who will not waste that capital and bring the firm to bankruptcy. If, on the other hand, it is *not* a

business in ever so small a degree, then you must
make women "independent factors," so that they
may not be tempted to go to the altar for the
bread that perisheth.

I am quite aware that there is a third suggestion
lying on the debatable ground between the two
theories. It is this, that every woman's power of
household management is her natural capital; that
if her husband brings the money and she brings
the domestic work, she contributes her fair share
to a firm which is partly spiritual, partly material;
that God himself created this allotment, and that
it is the *real* theory of marriage.

Immense weight should be given to this suggestion, because it is eminently true for the lower
classes, where the married woman ought not to be
the actual bread-winner.* It ought also to be
true for a much larger portion of the middle class

* Although not strictly incidental to the subject, I should
like to observe in passing, that no wise thinkers, however
anxious to extend the spheres of employment for women, are
satisfied with the state of things among the working classes
which tempts the mothers of families away from their homes;
and this on the plain and simple principle that a person who
undertakes a responsible duty to another human being, and

than will condescend to accept it.   It is absurd to
keep servants and to bring daughters up to idleness and penury, unable to do household work,
and disgusted at the idea of marrying in a rank
where it would be necessary to do it.   The way in
which all girls who can possibly be supported in
idleness shrink from real active household work, is
a great mistake and a great misfortune; it does
not help their intellectual development the least in

to society at large, is bound to fulfil it. It is a matter of
moral honesty, as well as of sentiment, and it would be very
wholesome if it were so judged. The various degrees of external occupation which a mother can undertake ought likewise to be measured by the same standard. A great singer,
an artist, or an author, who keeps good servants, may righte-
ously afford the number of hours necessary to fulfil her profession, without any sacrifice of the welfare of her children,
and there are innumerable excellent women who have combined these avocations and duties with irreproachable exactitude; but, in the working class, where the mother is also
nurse and house-servant, where all the cleanliness, economy,
and comfort of a home depend on her actual and constant
superintendence, her absence at any trade is as bad in a money
as in a moral point of view. The frightful mortality among
children who are left to the care of youthful inefficient nurses,
the accidents by fire and water and dangerous falls, sufficiently indicate the sanitary evils connected with the mother's
absence. I was told the other day of an abominable practice

the world; they would be a great deal cleverer and
healthier and happier if they did it; and if poor
middle-class fathers would bring up their little
daughters to do the house work, after the fashion
of Mary in the " Minister's Wooing," and pay the
money they would otherwise give to a servant for
wages and board, to an assurance office to secure
their daughters dowries, it would be a great deal
the better plan in innumerable cases, and plenty of
occasionally pursued by ignorant mothers when leaving their
children for the day; namely, tying a bit of sponge which
had been previously dipped in some narcotic into an infant's
mouth for it to suck! A very certain method of keeping the
poor little thing quiet during its hours of loneliness! As regards economy, it is insisted upon by those who have most
thoroughly studied the application of working men's wages,
that if the husband is in full work, the wife's absence from
home causes an actual loss, for which her earnings by no
means compensate; in other words, that the "penny saved"
in her household management is actually *more* than the
"penny gained" by her labour. It is easy to believe this,
but even if it were not true, the disorganisation caused by the
housewife's absence from the working man's home, the dirt,
discomfort, hurry, and ill-prepared meals, are more than
sufficient reasons why every woman who has deliberately
chosen to take upon herself certain heavy moral obligations,
should fulfil them scrupulously to the exclusion of all temptations in other directions.

time would remain for mental cultivation, though less for shabby and showy accomplishments.

But such an idea is widely removed from any-body's thoughts or practice at present, and the actual fact staring us in the face is, that young men do *not* seek portionless wives, and do *not* con-sider the present amount of domestic knowledge and practice owned by young women as equivalent to " capital." Therefore we are obliged to put aside this third suggestion as being of no real use in regard to those included as " educated women."

Since, therefore, such are exonerated by custom and by the altered habits of society from those active domestic habits which make a woman in the lower ranks an equal sharer in her husband's labours, and enable her in single life to make a little money go a long way, and since public opinion nominally condemns marriage for a main-tenance, where is the practicable alternative, ex-cept to help her to become an " independent factor " on a higher level? It is very easy to cast a dexterous colour of ridicule over people and things by a happy epithet, which seems to embody a new idea in words, and to point out its absurdity; but let us just consider what an independent factor really is, and who come fairly under that designation.   In the first place, all domestic servants, * the nurse, the cook, and the housemaid, without whom we are accustomed to think that we could not exist for a day, are women working on their own account and away from their own homes, yet we do not find that tradesmen consider them unlikely to make good wives.   Again, all dressmakers, shopkeepers, charwomen, &c., earn an independent livelihood before marriage, and in many cases continue to do so afterwards, yet we never heard a word about the unfitness of their pursuits, or any tendency in these to separate them from the men of their own rank.   The real truth is, that very nearly three-fourths of the adult unmarried women of this country, above the age of twenty, *are* independent factors ; that they marry easily and happily from this position, and continue their work or discontinue it according to their individual circumstances, the number of their children, and

* According to the census of 1851, the female domestic servants numbered 664,467 ; in 1861, they numbered 976,931.

various considerations which cannot be reduced to any rule. Therefore we are arguing about a very small, though very important proportion of the whole body of women, and it is absurd to deal with the question as if it were a desperate, hopeless, and anomalous hitch in our social welfare.

To hear the remarks made by very clever and very kind people about this subject, it would be easy to fancy that some *bouleversement* of the whole nature and duties of women had become a lamentable necessity. The more I think about it, the more sure I feel that this notion is an utter exaggeration. I believe that the particular evil we are now trying so earnestly to remove is the growth of modern times, and closely connected with the growth of the middle class. As civilisation has increased during the last century, a number of women have been uplifted by the labours of men into a sphere where considerable cultivation and a total abnegation of household work have become a custom and a creed, but no corresponding provision has been made for them of occupation in the higher and more intellectual fields of work. They share, through their male relatives, in all the vicissitudes

to which individual members of the middle class
are subject; and they are helplessly dependent on
these turns of the tide, having been trained to no
method of self-help. All that seems to me to be
wanted is that the women of the middle classes,
belonging to professional or to commercial families, should heartily accept the life of those
classes, instead of aping the life of the aristocracy.

Daughters living idly at home while their parents
cannot hope to leave them a maintenance, are in
fact the *exceptions* in our busy, respectable female
population. Let them shrink from creating an
exceptional class of paupers, and take up their lot
with the rest of their sisters, finding such occupa-
tions as will call out and employ their better education. I cannot see why working ladies need be
more unsexed than working housemaids, nor why
that activity, which is deemed to make a woman
eligible as a wife to a working man, should, when
exercised on higher subjects, unfit and discredit
her to be the wife of a working barrister or medical
man.

But it is little use to argue against ideas of caste
which are so deeply rooted in our middle classes,

unless some wise and active measures are also taken to change the current.

This brings me to the third great want which seems to me to hinder women from possessing themselves of a fair share of the domain of business : the want of efficient female superintendence in all those trades and offices in which women might otherwise be employed. If lack of capital prevents grown-up daughters from leaving home and starting for themselves, lack of what they consider due and proper protection certainly weighs heavily with parents against parting with young girls, allowing them to be apprenticed to a trade or hired as clerks. In the minds of many men, this is an objection never to be got over, and no one who has any experience of life will wonder at it. It is evident that the conditions of business life can, therefore, never be identical for men and for women ; no sane person will tolerate the notion of flinging girls into those very temptations and dangers which we lament and regret for boys ; and those who rise from the ranks into the middle class show the change in no more marked manner than in the standard of decorum they require from the gentle sex. If mothers are often less stringent than fathers, it is rather because they know less of what external life is, than because they would shrink less from exposing their daughters to evil example. Therefore we may talk to the wind about the folly of bringing up girls to be governesses, unless we so arrange that every woman is protected in the exercise of her profession almost as well as she would be if teaching by some domestic hearth. Nor is it any answer to say that some women, ten, twenty, or a hundred, have struggled nobly with the toughest problems of outer life. That Rosa Bonheur and Elizabeth Blackwell and Harriet Hosmer studied their professions in the general arena is very true and very inspiring, and makes one think well of one's kind, both men and women; but even their stories will never persuade the ordinary father to send his ordinary daughter out unprotected into the world of competition; and I think it very well that it is so. We should, therefore, exercise a little common sense in arranging all those workshops and offices in which girls work, and we should invariably associate them with older women; they should in all cases work in companies together,

and not intermixed with men, and so long as they
are young they must be under some definite charge.
This has been managed in the collegiate institutions now so generally in vogue for education; and
I believe it rests with the women of the upper
ranks to carry the principle down in minute rami-
fications into every department of woman's work.
Let those who have birth, and leisure and means
at disposal, set themselves to consider how they
can make trade and professional life safe and respectable for young girls, and they will not find it
a very difficult task. I may be reproached for not
being willing to leave this matter to the natural
action of society; but I confess I do think it requires at first a little "benevolent" consideration
from those who do not work for their livelihood.
The prejudice to be got over in the minds of
parents is so deeply rooted, and their fears so well
founded, that I think the active interest of women
of high social rank would smooth the way very
much sooner than anything else. Many of them
are deeply in earnest about charities for. their own
sex, and will spend time and trouble and money
over schemes of less practical import. If they

would but give direct countenance to all such new
classes and workshops as are opened for those who
would otherwise be governesses, it would go a long
way to smoothe the change in the minds of men.

From the first days in which political economy
rose from the region of empirics into those of
science, a covert war has been waged as to how
far it expressed the whole truth in regard to social
wellbeing. The great laws which it defines stand
up like rocks amidst the wild waves of theory, and
compel them to retire, yet natures in whom love
and reverence predominate insist on supplement-
ing their shortcomings by a higher principle. No-
where is this tendency more clearly to be discerned
than in the writings of John Stuart Mill himself;
indeed, he occasionally retreats upon the moral
intuitions of the human heart in a way that exposes
him to censure from those who are willing to push
intellectual conclusions to their farthest limits.
The efforts made by the Christian socialist party
are striking examples of attempts to interweave
religious and economical law ; and the necessity of
allowing other considerations than those of science
to rule our actions is shown with peculiar clearness

by the social phenomena which accompany the introduction of machinery into any trade previously worked by hand. In the long run, every such trade ends by employing many more hands at increased wages, but the immediate effect is, to throw numbers of the old workers out of employ; and as human beings do not easily migrate from county to county, much less from country to country, and as, moreover, the grown man and woman cannot easily learn a new trade, even though such may be actually waiting for them in a fresh place, the immediate and invariable result of the introduction of machinery is a large amount of human distress, including hunger and cold, and other very real griefs. Therefore no manufacturer who is not influenced by selfish greed will introduce machinery where it was not previously in use, without taking pains to ease the transition to his workpeople. In like manner, every effort ought just now to be made in aid of female emigration; for the sewing-machine is destroying daily the wretched profession of the seamstress, to the great future benefit of the sex, but to the immediate anguish and destitution of the lowest class of worker.

L

And so I believe that, though the opening of new paths to educated women will be a very great economical benefit, I see plainly that we have great moral interests also at stake, which require to be jealously guarded, that we may not look to the political economy of the question only, but must take anxious care to build up the new theory in connexion with the old reverence for all that makes a woman estimable; in gaining somewhat, we must not lose more. Therefore let us call on Englishwomen of social station to impart to this movement just that element of moral repute which it will eminently require to ensure it from failure; let them weigh well the precious material out of which working women are to be made, and not leave the introduction of educated girls into business to the chances of the business world alone. Almost everything depends on the moral tone communicated from the headquarters of each separate sphere of employment. Just as in the beginning of this century fiction was redeemed from its coarseness and absurdity by Sir Walter Scott and Miss Edgeworth, and a small contemporaneous knot of writers; so the professions, art, and literature re-

ceive in every age the powerful stamp of a few
leading minds. On the ten or twenty women in
England who during the next dozen years may rise
into eminence in any new sphere for their sex, will
depend an incalculable amount of good or evil to
our whole class of youthful educated workers. If
such twenty maintain their position in all that is
"fair and lovely and of good report," and if they
be well supported by those of their own sex whose
names are an assured guarantee to the whole kingdom ; if ladies who are exempt from the necessity
of working will associate on terms of equality with
ladies who are *not*, just as a baronet and a barrister
are now for all conventional purposes of equal
rank, then we shall see this "new theory," as its
opposers like to call it, carried triumphantly over
every rock and shoal. It will become a respectable and desirable thing for a woman to practise a
profession or a business, just as it has already become a respectable and a desirable thing for a
woman to become a good poet, novelist, or artist.
In fine, it will no longer be half a disgrace for a
lady to become an "independent factor" in any
other post but that of a governess.

If such hearty and generous pains be not taken, then the economical change (being of itself inevitable) will be worked out with peril and difficulty to the happiness of the community. But of this there is little fear. I rejoice to feel, from daily experience, how wide and warm is the sympathy of women with women, when once excited. I believe that all honour from their own sex awaits those who achieve distinction in any branch of work, and that those who make up their minds to seize the first opportunity that opens to them of pursuing any avocation, however humble, will find in future that their social *caste* is dependent on what they are, and not on the occupation in which they may happen to be engaged.

VII.

CO-OPERATION.

CO-OPERATION.

OME of the difficulties likely to hinder women from entering successfully into business may be much lessened by the application of the principles of co-operation. If the strain of competition be productive of evil to workers of the stronger sex, causing an over-tax of health, strength, and energy, tempting to late hours, and daring speculation, we may reasonably regard the business career of women as more likely to be injured by the same causes, and regard the new and fertile principle which has already created some very flourishing enterprises in retail trade, with a hopeful eye.

Believing that it may be turned to excellent account by industrious women, let us begin at the beginning, and define, in the simplest words, what co-operation is ; premising that, among political

economists, John Stuart Mill stands pre-eminent
as its apostle, and that the principle, for the sake of
which he perhaps in former years slightly damaged
his scientific reputation among men of a narrower
school, may now, having fought its way year by
year, through some failure and a few disgraces, be
considered fairly established.

Co-operation, in the commercial sense, implies
an application of the joint-stock principle; that the
money with which a concern—say a grocer's shop,
or a tailor's business, or even a factory—is carried
on, has been clubbed together by different people,
who appoint a manager and share the profits.
This is what we usually mean by co-operation in
trade, and it is not true and real unless the shares
are actually shares *owned* by different hands.   For
instance, if a committee of benevolent people set
to work to benefit any class of sufferers, or to improve the condition of any class of artisans, and if
this committee collect subscriptions and distribute
relief, or even if it organises self-supporting plans,
it is still not a *co-operative* body in the trade sense
of the word.

There must be a joint-stock, a common fund,

clubbed together, yet nominally divided and actually divisible ; just as A, B, C, and D might own
a great cask of wine, so many quarts to each. And
this common fund may be used or divided in various ways ; the shares may be equal or unequal; the
government of the different parts of the concern
may be federal or strictly democratic ; and so on.
Only it is necessary that there shall be shares and
proportionate profits, and that in some way the concern shall be self-governed.

Self-government is the root of the idea, for which
reason Mr Mill says, " *The peculiar characteristic, in
short, of civilised beings, is the capacity of co-operation.*"

And this refers to all moral as well as to all
commercial co-operation.   The savage cannot co-
operate in a sphere higher than that of the yelling
war-dance.   The submissive hordes of Eastern des-
potisms were ranged in ranks under one master, but
they did not cohere in mutual activity.   There are
two conditions under which men associate firmly :
the influence of intellectual ideas and moral feel-
ings, such as swayed the Greek communities and
the Roman republic ; and of *religion*, which fuses
the will of many into one.

Even amidst Pagan nations these combined secular and religious influences have sufficed to create
vigorous social life. But the triumph of co-operation in its more extended moral sense was reserved
for Christianity to declare. The commerce of
Christian Europe,—of Venice, of Florence, of
Holland, showed it in the middle ages in a secular
form ; the countless pious orders for conversion,
for teaching, and for solace, showed it in a religious
aspect. In the English Church every day sees
some fresh attempt at active combination ; and the
Methodist "class meetings" express the same need.

It is not without design that I refer to the more
strictly moral and religious meaning of the word,
because it lies at the basis of the commercial one.
Before people can take shares in a coal-mine, appoint a manager, and divide the profits, they must
be able to trust each other and the man whom they
appoint ; they must agree on the principles of trade,
and keep their tempers one towards the other. It is,
therefore, easy to see that when civil peace is established, and trade principles are pretty much the same
in every town, and merchants and traders find their
transactions can go on from year to year in peace

and quietness, they will naturally begin to think whether they cannot apply the principle of united action to greater profit.

"*Accordingly, there is no more certain incident of the progressive change taking place in society, than the continual growth of the principle and practice of co-operation.*"

Without entering too deeply into the history of the question, we will consider the reasons which first turned the minds of speculative men in this direction ; the first of which is the immense importance now attaching to the production of wealth. It is quite a modern idea, at least in its modern sense. Of course individuals at all times liked riches ; plenty to eat, to drink, and to spend ; but if they failed to acquire them they acquiesced more quietly than they do now. Commerce ran more in a groove : there was a commercial class, and there were commercial cities *par excellence.* Every city is now commercial, or struggling to become so. The modern idea of capital was formerly pretty much confined to Jews and Lombards, and burghers of the middle class. Now, every gentleman considers how he may best lay his out to advantage.

But what is the result of money thus rolling over
and over, and accumulating like a snowball at every
revolution? There is immensely more gold, also
more meat and drink and clothes; and yet somehow the distribution among the increased population is not quite satisfactory; since Professor Faw-
cett reckons that the labourer has not as much to
eat and drink as he had in the reign of Henry VIII.
The money and the food must lie somewhere *in
drifts;* and as neither the aristocracy of rank nor
the aristocracy of trade can eat and drink and
wear more than a limited amount in a year, it be-
hoves us to seek some method of spreading the
necessaries of life over a larger class. When we
begin to investigate causes, it appears that one
great power underlies all modern trade—the power
of capital. Plenty of capital, absolute security for
that capital, and rapid contrivances to make that
capital turn round and double itself at every turn,
these are the Articles of Trade.

Now mark the result : the man with capital is
not merely a *double* man, but a *tenfold* man : he is
not merely a man and money, but a moneyed man.
His power has increased in a geometrical ratio.

If you want the proof it lies in this, that a man with £100,000 can use up the labour of say five thousand of his fellow-creatures, paying *them* a fraction of what he gets *himself.*

Yet what is to be done? His advantage is perfectly fair. He saved his money, and his money has made him equal to ten men. He has made a huge lever, and of course he can lift immense weights. If he chooses to buy up the Highlands and turn off the cottars, you can hardly interfere with him under the present laws of property; and if he takes a freak and shuts up his mill, the workmen must go to the union. Of course it is very unlikely that he will do anything very unreasonable. He has his interests and also his character to consult; and it is possible that he is one of the best of men, and that he and his family are doing all they can for the comfort and instruction of the workpeople. All I wish to point out is, that he actually does possess an enormous power; that thousands of his fellow creatures are in his hand; and that, in the words of a French thinker, *les barons de la Feodalité* are only replaced by *les barons de l'Industrie.*

What, then, can be done to balance this new
power? It may be said that in a free country all
men are free to save, and take an even chance of
becoming capitalists. It is true that they are so
far on an equality; yet would it not be far better
if, instead of having, as now, an equal chance of
standing on a summit, all honest and industrious
men could calculate on a more even remuneration,
and be raised to a higher level?

This problem has engaged the attention of many
acute intellects and benevolent hearts during this
century, and they seem to be agreed on one point
—namely, that any return to production on a small
scale is become impossible. "A people," ob-
serves Mr Mill, "who have once adopted the
large system of production, either in manufactures or in agriculture, are not likely to recede from
it; nor when population is kept in due proportion
to the means of support, is there any sufficient reason why they should. Labour is unquestionably
more productive on the system of large industrial
enterprises : the produce, if not greater absolutely,
is greater in proportion to the labour employed : the
same number of persons can be supported equally

well with less toil and greater leisure ; which will be wholly an advantage as soon as civilisation and improvement have so far advanced that what is a benefit to the whole shall be a benefit to each individual composing it. The problem is, to obtain the efficiency and economy of production on a large scale, without dividing the producers into two parties with hostile interests, employers and employed, the many who do the work being mere servants under the command of the one who supplies the funds, and having no interest of their own in the enterprise, except to fulfil their contract and earn their wages."

The joint-stock principle is capable of solving this problem, and is now rapidly becoming recognised by all classes of trades. But its battles have been most severe, partly on account of its apparently democratic tendency, partly because it early became mixed up with moral and social questions with which it has properly no necessary concern. It was successively associated in the public mind with the St Simonians, the Fourierites, and the disciples of Robert Owen ; the followers of the three systems of social philosophy, though they by no means agreed among themselves, all united in appreciating the value of co-operation in every department of life, and as their moral theories were strongly opposed both to religion and to common sense, a kindred slur attached itself to the principle of associated labour upon which their speculations reposed as a basis. Its inherent truth, however, gradually caused it to make way. Experiments were tried and found to answer; an application of it was made by a house-painter in Paris, a M. Leclaire, who published an account of his system of operation as early as 1842. Many other co-operative establishments have been formed during the last twenty years in Paris, and their commercial success has been signal, although being more or less worked by men who came into prominence in 1848, they have succeeded *sous la rose,*—and less has been heard about them than would otherwise have been the case.

But, strange to say, it is in England, Conservative England, that the great triumphs have been achieved, and that the joint-stock *principle* has quietly invaded all parts of trade, while it is in England also that co-operation, in the stricter sense, has received its most striking development. In proof of the first assertion look at the joint-stock companies now in vogue for every purpose, from the building of the Great Eastern to the supplying of the public with pure tea. Every railway company is joint-stock, and joint-stock banks are in every town. The late Limited Liability Act afforded a protection to companies which had long been granted in France, and enabled many to be started which it would otherwise have been impossible to attempt, since a dozen people will easily be found to risk £100 each, and *that only*, who would not risk their whole fortune on anything which they could not constantly inspect and efficiently control. Thus it is that Mr Mill says, "*Associations of individuals voluntarily combining their small contributions, now perform works, both of an industrial and of many other characters, which no one person, or small number of persons, are rich enough to accomplish, or for the performance of which the few persons capable of accomplishing them were formerly enabled to exact the most inordinate remuneration.*" His further prediction, that " as wealth increases and business capacity improves, we may look forward to

M

a great extension of establishments both for industrial and other purposes, formed by the collective
contributions of large numbers," is in daily process
of accomplishment ; and I would now draw attention to the gradual growth among us of co-operative societies in the stricter sense of the word.
The most signal success has been achieved by the
Rochdale Mill, which rose from such small beginnings to so great a result as to have excited
general interest.

" The society dates from 1844.   It originated
in the efforts of a few weavers to better a condition which chartism, strikes, communism, and
other pretentious agencies, left pretty much as
they found it.   By dividing the town into districts,
and appointing collectors, the committee of management combined to scrape together somewhere
about £36.   A third of the sum collected was
spent on some absolutely necessary fixtures and
shop apparatus, there being left about £24 where-
with to buy in a stock to begin business.   They
rented a shop at £10 per annum.   The credit
system, which had foundered all preceding attempts, was most resolutely avoided.   All pur-

chases and all sales were for ready money, or
'brass,' as it is called in Yorkshire; no matter
what were the exigencies, or what the character
of buyers, down they must lay the brass on the
counter before an article could be removed.
Originally the store was opened only at certain
hours, but in 1851 it was opened all day, a regular
superintendent and shopmen being appointed.

"At the end of 1858 the Equitable Pioneers'
Co-operative Society consisted of 1950 members,
and the funds amounted to £18,160, 5s. 4d.
The business done during the year was £71,689,
and the profits made £6284, 17s. 4½d. The
average weekly receipt was £1600. We have to
add a still more interesting fact. Two and a half
per cent. off net profits were, by the constitution
of the society, devoted to what are termed educa-
tional purposes; properly speaking, the support of
the library and reading-room. The library now
contains 3000 volumes of useful and entertaining
literature; the tables of the reading-room are
covered with papers, and the loan of books and
the perusal of papers are alike free to the members." Thus far Mr Chambers's recent inquiry

fully confirms the accuracy of his account; but justice requires the statement that this society, like most of the attempts at co-operative stores and manufactories during the last twenty-five years, have originated amongst men who were formerly communists of the school of Robert Owen—who, undaunted by many failures, have retained their faith in the co-operative principle until they have achieved success. The societies are the solid and practicable remnant of the teaching of Robert Owen, and are proof of the wisdom of attempting only such improvement at any time as society is fit for and can appreciate. Owen's proposed economical arrangements did not fit in; the required change was too great, and the result was failure. In June 1844, says one of the most active members of the Rochdale Society, it was believed that no member could or would subscribe more than 2d. per week per share; and when one offered to lay down 2s. 6d. and another 5s., the offers caused great surprise, and some consternation was evident when an enthusiastic member offered to venture 20s.

Now the applicability of this principle to female

labour is evident. A business managed on the co-operative plan is deprived of most of its strain, for the simple reason that the custom of the shareholders is secured. This is the gist of the whole matter, the middleman is done away with, and his profit is saved. The same people who buy in wholesale, sell out retail to each other, and of course there is a surplus to be divided. If twenty people club together to purchase food or clothing wholesale, and agree to purchase what they each personally require at the ordinary retail price which they would pay in any other shop, of course they create a business yielding profit. This profit is found by repeated experience to be sufficient for all the working expenses, of manager, clerks, shoproom, all according to the scale on which the society works, and a per centage on shares besides. If there are a great many shareholders, there will be a great deal of custom, and many assistants employed. If there are very few shareholders, the object must be to keep all the working expenses as low as possible, so that as much as possible of the difference between wholesale and retail expenditure may be divided.

If twenty ladies in any town would club together
£5 a piece, they might open a stationery shop in
which, if they gave all their own custom and tried
to get that of their friends, they might secure a
profit after employing a lady as manager, and if the
business increased, female clerks also.   The same
principle might be applied to grocery and drapery,
and to other articles of common consumption;
but it would be a mistake to apply it to very costly
and seldom needed wares, as the profits of course
depend on a regular and sufficient custom, and a
quick turning of the capital employed.   The result
of such an experiment, carried out with economy,
discretion, and good temper, would be found to be
surprising in its results.

VIII.

WORKS OF BENEVOLENCE.

WORKS OF BENEVOLENCE.

HIS subject has been so amply treated of by writers possessing practical acquaintance with its details, that though, in its widest sense, it is, in my judgment, more important and more interesting than any other, it would be superfluous and almost impertinent to speak of it in this book, except in its economical aspect. To say nothing of continental labours and sources of information—to say nothing of the vast and efficient organisations of the Church of Rome, we have had in England Mrs Jameson, Florence Nightingale, Mary Carpenter, Louisa Twining, Dr Howson, Mr Ludlow, and many more, writing of this portion of woman's work in almost every point of view from which it can be regarded, except perhaps that on which I purpose to touch, the relief of the labour

market by the drafting off of the most reliable
candidates into these works.   Even unpaid religious communities relieve the labour market.   It
is very true that each individual worker is a disin-
terested volunteer, but it is equally true that wherever the system is really organised, all the workers
are fed, clothed, and supported in old age in the
cheapest manner from the funds of the institution,
and thus constitute a very important part of the
paid labour of the country.   Those who are rich
bring or leave fortunes to the community ; but
excellent and valuable workers are often taken in
without money, or with a smaller portion ; and
thus, regarding the question on its purely economical side, they give their labour for a permanent
maintenance.   When, therefore, we read in Mrs
Jameson's pages of the Paris hospitals, including
the Lariboissière, founded by a rich lady, and
employing twenty-five Sisters of Charity, of the
hospitals at Vienna, at Milan, at Vervelli and Turin,
all under the superintendence of sisters, and all
benefiting in the most undeniable manner by such
care, insomuch that in one instance, where they
were expelled in 1848, they had to be recalled to

save the hospital from almost cureless ruin, we must remember that there is an economical as well as a religious side to women's work in community, and that many of these sisters represent in continental countries the class which with us is composed of wretched superannuated governesses.

To those who object to the idea of religious communities, it may be said that much of the same material benefit would be secured by giving remunerative labour to women not only in our charitable institutions, but in those under the control of the Poor Law Boards. That some such change is urgently needed for the sake of the *inmates*, is now becoming allowed on all hands. The moral question has made immense strides during the last ten years, thanks to many good women's words and works.

The employing of educated women in such posts of importance is partly an official, partly a private question. Mrs Jameson strove hard to get Government to recognise the need, so have the other ladies mentioned above, each in their separate department; but there are in England immense organisations for benevolence as well as for industry, which are quite independent of Government, though the numbers of human beings with which they deal raise them into national importance; for instance, there are all the great hospitals, whose funds are collected and managed by committees, and whose requirements in the way of female work are so great and complicated that they would demand a separate chapter; and there are the thousands upon thousands of workers in factory life, for whom due superintendence would create a new moral state. Without entering into the merits or demerits of the system,—a system which some most intelligent thinkers earnestly deprecate on sanitary and moral grounds,—it is evident that, as thousands of women and children *are* working within factory walls at this very hour, it is most important that everything should be done, not only to improve their condition, but to prevent their actual deterioration. Now this cannot be done by schools alone. To educate the new generation aright is a great matter: but even for that which is now acting or working on earth there is much to be done, and the mothers of the rising generation can be taught how to train their little ones in all that concerns the bodily health and the spiritual culture of the earliest years. A keen eye and a practised intellect are invaluable when brought to bear on the needs of the artisan, and in the thousand details of domestic life, a *woman's* eye and a *woman's* intellect are indisputably more available than a man's. Nobody, for instance, doubts that the clergyman's wife and the district visitor have a very distinct and important part to play in a parish ; a part supplied in Catholic countries by the Sœurs de Charité. To whom will the woman of the working class come to tell a thousand petty troubles except to a woman? Who can judge whether the meat has been made the most of, or the stuff " cut to waste," except a woman ; and who is likely to be told of the difficulties and disgraces which sooner or later touch every widely connected household, except a woman? To whom will a mother speak of her wandering daughter, or her scapegrace son, except a woman? I do not deny that the clergyman and the minister may do an immense work, nor that they combine many of the feminine with the masculine virtues by reason of their special training. But I think all my readers must acknowledge that a vast deal is still left to the woman's peculiar province; and that where hundreds of women are gathered together in any employ, it is very wise to introduce among them the missionary labour of their own sex. And though we all allow that "Bible women," and Christian workers of every class, however humble, may act beneficially on the population, we have not enough of them, and it is still evident, even with regard to themselves, that in no case is the superintending activity of educated women more urgently demanded.

I know of three cases in which it has been tried; perhaps my readers may be able to furnish other instances from their own memories. The first was at Halstead, in Essex, at the silk mill belonging to the Messrs Courtauld, where a lady was employed for fourteen years in visiting the homes of the workers, and in exercising a general superintendence over the schools.*

The second was at Birmingham, under totally

* See "Experience of Factory Life," by M. M. Sold at the Office of the Society for Promoting the Employment of Women, 19 Langham Place, London, W.

different and far more unfavourable conditions:
men and women are mixed together in the workshops of that town; the trades are in many instances very rough and dirty, and the lady who
attempted to organise a factory-home there seems
to have felt her attempt almost a failure, and the
conditions of factory labour, as carried on in that
town, destructive to the soul and body. Still, if
this be true, all the more need for her presence
and inspection.

The third experiment was tried at a mill near
Cheadle, where the master's wife co-operated
warmly with the lady employed.

The great advantage, in an economical point of
view, of using up the sort of mind required for benevolent work is, that its faculties, though of the very
highest kind, lie in the normal order. There will probably always be something exceptional in the class
of women fitted to be successful artists or authors,
even more so than among men; but for the matron
of an hospital, the superintendent of factory workers,
the authority over the interior of an hospital, we do
not want clever people in the common sense of the
word; we want mature women, whether single,

married, or widowed, possessing firmness, discretion, and experience of life. If a candidate possess these, she will soon learn the technicalities of her new occupation ; and if she do not possess these all other acquirements will prove useless. Just the women who have been educated by *life* are needed, women trained as it were by Providence for the work ; yet how many of these lack the special knowledge of the governess, have no genius for art, and would be utterly wasted on any mere industrial pursuit.

Singularly enough, though the aptitudes of women for high professional success are frequently doubted, and are indeed only illustrated by a few prominent examples in each department, their capacities of government and organisation are not doubted by any one who has taken the pains to write or read history. Some of the most remarkable, and indeed some of the most formidable and unscrupulous sovereigns, have been of the female sex ; religious orders have been created, organised, and for centuries ruled by women ; every age has produced numerous examples of the woman born to administer, with her keys dangling at her girdle. Notice that there is nothing in the slightest degree un-feminine in the picture. A poem can be written, and a fresco painted, to delineate her excellences. She can even be treated in sculpture : clay will lend itself to the modelling, marble will not refuse to embody her ; nay, such a character is carved in alabaster upon many a Gothic tomb. This is a subtle test of fitness ; art recoils from the unfit, the unnatural ; beauty declines to adorn the figure which no true usefulness ennobles.

IX.

MEANS OF EDUCATION.

MEANS OF EDUCATION.

THE means of education furnished to women of the upper classes have, for the most part, been of a strictly private nature, but it would be, in my judgment, wrong to infer that they have been therefore less efficient for their purpose. Wherever European society has attained to ease and luxury, much pains have been taken with the education of daughters ; stress is often laid upon the learned women of the middle ages, but the last century furnishes us with abundance of French and English memoirs, showing that, if less proficient in the classical languages, yet that the average of general culture among ladies of the upper class was a fair one. Their letters furnish us with incontestable proof. A curious example of this is found in the volumes recently published in France upon Marie Antoinette, which give a

complete denial to the assertion of a well-known
English writer, that Marie Theresa was too much
occupied with affairs of state to attend properly to
the education of her children ; also that the young
Dauphine on her arrival in France spoke "imperfect
French." We now possess the original correspondence between Marie Antoinette and her sister
Christine ; the letters are written in French, which
was the family language. She recalls her "tutor, the
Abbé Metastasio," whom she says she liked better
than all her other masters ; and one of her reasons
for loving the Princesse de Lamballe was that she
was an Italian, and spoke the sweet language of
Italy to her. The letters, though they contain no
allusions to science or history, are the letters of a
vigorous, well-cultivated mind. It may seem hardly
worth while to cite this one example of popular
misconception, but sometimes one example furnishes a type of a mistake, for Marie Antoinette
has been considered quick, clever, and "frivolous"
for seventy long years, the very model of the noble-
woman of the last century. In England, Mrs
Delany was not a very clever woman—neither an
authoress nor a *belle-esprit*—yet look at her corres-

pondence. Of the private education of this century, it seems to me we have cause to think well, considering that the object to be attained in regard to female training is a general balance and sound culture, rather than technical proficiency in certain branches of knowledge. As more distinct paths and professions open to women, in accordance with the social tendencies of the day, of course provision must be made for their being furnished with the special knowledge requisite to such ends. But this is not what has hitherto been desired, or desirable, nor for the majority of women will it ever be so ; what they want for the exigencies of life is sense, capacity, general intelligence ; and knowledge given to the mind, as food is given to the body, so as to make it strong and serviceable for its duties.

Although, however, private education is still the rule, the needs of modern society tend here, as in so many other departments, towards combined efforts. The number of girls who require an intellectual training is constantly on the increase, because middle-class families are rising into opulence on the one hand, and on the other from causes previously specified, more women are dependant on their own exertions than was the case in past generations. Hence the establishment of colleges, which, though they cannot be reckoned in the same category with those venerable abodes of learning which we associate with the word, are nevertheless a very marked advance upon any institutions yet set apart for women.

It is curious to observe that, while the ideas and the necessities of former ages did not as yet demand any combined efforts of the kind for themselves, women nevertheless contributed, and that largely, to the foundation and endowment of colleges for the use of men in both our old universities. At Oxford, Joan Davis, wife of a citizen of that town, gave certain estates for the establishment of " two logic lectures." In the thirteenth century, John de Baliol, dying suddenly before he had completed all his intentions in regard to the infant college which still bears his name, left no will, but verbally enjoined his wife and his executors to take care of the same. Lady Dervorgille (which was the name borne by the wife) accordingly devoted time and substance to the carrying out of her husband's wish, and showed no lack of generosity. In 1282 she appointed statutes, under her seal, which are curious as throwing light on the collegiate discipline of the period ; in 1284 she bought a tenement for the "sixteen poor scholars," and having repaired and enlarged it, gave it to them to dwell in. In the same year she gave them lands in the county of Northumberland, and got her son to confirm the statutes she had made ; so that to her faithful energy is owing the early stability of that work which her husband had only time to commence, and which yet remains after the lapse of six centuries a testimony of their united zeal. Still speaking of Oxford, Exeter College found a considerable donor in a Lady Shiers, and Queen Anne in like manner benefited Oriel. Queen's College was founded by Robert Eglesfield, confessor to Queen Phillippa, and it was aided by her, by Henrietta Maria, and by two queens of the house of Hanover. Wadham College was founded by Nicholas Wadham and his wife Dorothy, an eminent benefactor to several colleges in this university. Mr Wadham died before he had executed any part of his plan, which then devolved wholly on the said Dorothy. She bought the site of the ancient priory of Austin Friars, once a place of great distinction in the university, and on the 30th of July, in the year 1610, laid the first stone of the present college. She also promulgated the college statutes, which received the sanction of Parliament in 1612. The statues of her husband and herself yet adorn the walls. Among the benefactors of Worcester College is Mrs Sarah Eaton, who endowed seven fellowships and five scholarships for the sons of clergymen only.

Turning to the University of Cambridge, which contains thirteen colleges and four halls, we find that several were founded or assisted by women. Clare Hall was built in 1344 by Elizabeth de Burgh, heiress of the last Earl of Clare. By this lady it obtained its present name, with endowments for a master, ten fellows, and the same number of scholars. Pembroke Hall was founded by Mary, Countess of Pembroke, in 1343, and partially endowed. Margaret of Anjou founded and partially endowed Queen's College in 1448, and her rival, Elizabeth Woodville, completed it, for a master, nineteen fellows, and forty-five scholars. Christ's College, founded by Henry VI., was completely endowed by Margaret, Countess of Richmond and Derby; whose name is also perpetuated to this day by the "Lady Margaret Professorships" at St John's. Finally, Sidney Sussex College owes its existence to the bequests of Frances Sidney, Countess of Sussex.

After the large-sounding names of these time-honoured halls, the modest institutions founded for female advantage seem small enough; but it was only just to quote the liberal zeal of the women of history, who appreciated so well the advantages of education for others, that it is not reasonable to suppose they were themselves devoid of culture.

Of those superior schools, popularly known as Ladies' Colleges, the earliest in foundation, and in all respects the best known and most amply supported, is Queen's College, Harley Street, London, which was incorporated by royal charter in 1853 for the general education of ladies, and for granting certificates of knowledge. The first germs of this now flourishing institution are due, we believe, to the minds of the Revs. C. G. Nicholay and F. D. Maurice. "It was thought and felt," said Sir John Forbes, at the annual meeting of 1854, "that female

education in England was capable of receiving more
order, method, sequence, mutual support of one
part by the other, than any which it had yet obtained; above all, that it might be strengthened
and deepened, might be made to rest on broader
and securer bases, if the mental energies, intellec-
tually stronger and hitherto better cultivated, of the
man, were brought more immediately and directly
to bear on the female mind."

" At the beginning of the undertaking it was proposed to educate governesses, making the college
in fact a normal school of a high class; and in its
earlier years it maintained relations of intimacy
and alliance with that admirable institution . . . .
the Governesses' Benevolent Institution." This
connexion was, however, harmoniously dissolved;
the Crown granted a charter of incorporation, the
Queen allowed the college to be called by her
name, and founded in it a free scholarship during
her life. The Bishop of London accepted the
legally-constituted office of visitor, implying the exercise of a habitual authority and oversight on his
part; so that no nomination either to a seat in the
council or in the committee of education should

be valid without his sanction, and constituting him as the final arbiter in any appeal. The charter gave a council to the College, which elects the professors, teachers, and officers, and attends to the entire management of all financial arrangements. There is also a committee of education, consisting of the professors engaged in the different branches of tuition; and a considerable body of lady visitors, who regularly attend the classes,— one being present at every lecture and lessons delivered by the professors. The education given to the pupils is of a much higher order than that of the ordinary school, many first-rate men having given special courses of lectures, in addition to the teaching of the regular professors. Dr Whewell has delivered a course upon Plato; Mr Maurice upon the chief question which occupied the mind of Christendom from the fourteenth to the sixteenth century; Dr Stanley lately delivered a course upon Jewish History, and is one of the Board of Examiners, together with Dean Alford, the Rev. Derwent Coleridge, Mr Plumptre, and Mr Maurice.

The junior school connected with the college receives children under thirteen, and is numerously attended. Several scholarships have been founded, as follows :—The Professors' four, elected annually, founded by the Council in 1853, in consideration of £1500 paid by the professors towards expenses of the charter. The Maurice Scholarship, founded by subscription in 1854, to commemorate the services of the distinguished clergyman whose name it bears, as first chairman of the committee of education in the foundation and management of the college. This scholarship is tenable for two years, as also is that of the Lady Visitors. The Cambridge and Oxford Scholarships, the first founded by the Rev. T. A. Cock, the second by the Rev. Tullie Cornthwaite, are open to girls between the ages of thirteen and fifteen, who have lost their fathers, and are the children or grandchildren of Cambridge graduates or Oxford masters of arts. Certificates in special subjects are given at this college, such as in theology, mathematics, the physical sciences, mental and moral philosophy, English language and literature, Greek, Latin, and various other branches of learning.

The second institution of the kind which by its usefulness demands a description is the Ladies'

College in Bedford Square. Queen's College, Harley Street, may be considered to be a sort of offshoot to King's College, it having been founded and fostered by King's College men. This may be considered as standing in the same relation to the London University College. Queen's College is under the direct superintendence of the Bishop of London ; the Ladies' College is more secular, and represents what is commonly called the liberal interest or mixed education. It was founded in 1849, it being thought advisable to provide another college in another part of London, which might prove a centre for a fresh district. Many of the same people who had taken a vivid interest in the establishment of the first were concerned in that of the second, but the broad distinction of clerical and non-clerical has always been a marked one, though various clergymen have at different times been members of the executive council at Bedford Square. The general board consists of forty-nine persons, of whom twenty-eight are ladies and twenty-one are gentlemen. The executive council is composed of nine members, five of whom are gentlemen, having a gentleman for chairman, a

lady for honorary secretary. The college is divided
into senior and junior departments, the latter including pupils above nine and under fifteen. It
has developed admirably under the guidance of
the able superintendent, and numbers between
sixty and seventy children. In the senior department, young ladies (in many cases grown up
young women) are enabled either to pursue a
systematic course of study under the superintendence of the committee of education, in which case
they are called "students," or as pupils, to select
any number of special classes.

Several other colleges, possessing more or less of
corporate constitution, have been established in London and in the provincial towns, varying in their
character between the chartered dignity of Queen's
College and the classes of a superior day-school.
The distinctive features of these institutions are
the increased range of subject, and that male professors of far higher order are employed. When
Latin, Greek, and mathematics were to be learned,
it was needful to seek the assistance of men ; and,
on the other hand, highly educated men, sharing
in the domestic influences of their time, and accus-

tomed to see women learning under disadvantages
at home, responded to the appeal in many cases
with the zeal of volunteers ; and the sex which, in
times past, was far more anxious to afford the
means of education to the "poor scholars" of
Oxford and Cambridge than to supply its own
wants, now sees the tide turning in its favour. Nor
is this true of the Ladies' College alone. The
Female School of Art in Queen Square, under the
superintendence of Miss Gann, receives excellent
instruction from men ; the Working Women's College, in the same locality, is partly served by male
teachers, who come after their own day's avocations
are ended to give gratuitous help. In connexion
with these various efforts to improve female education, must be named the endeavour to provide
external and independent tests and certificates of
the instruction given in these schools and colleges.
Applications have been made for the extension to
girls of the Oxford and Cambridge examinations
for students who are not members of the university.
A special syndicate was appointed at Cambridge
to consider the subject, and they have made a

o

report recommending a scheme of examination
for girls, which was adopted (March, 1865) in
the Senate by a majority of fifty-five against fifty
votes.

At the University of Edinburgh a scheme of local
examinations, similar to that of the English universities, has just been instituted, and will come into
operation in June, under which girls and boys will
be examined on the same conditions.

An experimental examination, held by permission
of the syndicate of the University of Cambridge in
connexion with the general system of local middle-
class examination, took place in London rather
more than a year ago, and four of the pupils of
Queen's College obtained certificates. "Whether
the University," says Mr Plumptre, in his report, "will sanction the repetition of the experiment, or be so far satisfied with the result of
that already made, as to adopt the extension of
its examining machinery to girls as part of its
permanent system, we do not know; but we
venture to express our belief that, by so doing
it would materially forward the accomplishment

of the objects aimed at by the founders of this
college, and give to many schools for girls throughout England a higher standard of excellence, and
a stronger motive for aiming at it than they have
had hitherto."

X.

SOCIAL ECONOMY.

SOCIAL ECONOMY.

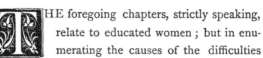HE foregoing chapters, strictly speaking, relate to educated women ; but in enumerating the causes of the difficulties which surround them in these days, I laid great stress on the industrial changes which have affected the lower classes, and I am unwilling to close without saying a few especial words on this subject. It would require a separate book to deal properly with the details of woman's part in mechanical industry according to the last census. Ten years ago, the census of 1851 was thus analysed, and the result appeared in an admirable book from a man's hand, entitled, " The Industrial and Social Position of Women in the Middle and Lower Ranks ; " and published by Messrs Chapman and Hall. The writer, however, takes a more favourable view of the moral results of the industrial

revolution than I can do, although, when I first
began investigating the subject, I was inclined to
share his opinion.

At this threshold of the question we are met by
two distinct theories, upon neither of which is it
possible to speak or act exclusively; and yet it will
make a great difference to our speech and to our
action, whether, in the depths of intellectual and
moral conviction, we abide by the one or the other
theory. Putting the matter as shortly and simply
as possible, Do we *wish* to see the majority of
women getting their own livelihood; or do we wish
to see it provided for them by men? Are we trying to assist the female population of this country
over a time of difficulty; or are we trying to develop a new state and theory of social life? I feel
bound to say that I regard the industrial question
from a temporary point of view, and that I should
greatly regret any change in the public opinion of
all classes, which would tend to make the men of
this country more unmindful of the material welfare
of the women of their families. Once infuse into
their minds the idea that they may fairly leave
women to shift for themselves, and that which is

now a necessity, or an accident, will become the natural rule. I should not complain of this if it could be proved, if it could even be imagined, that the chances of remunerative labour could be for all women what they are for all men; and that nature has adapted them for equal efforts in the race of competition. But the contrary is so evident as to render argument useless. Nobody thinks better of women than I do; or entertains greater respect for the large qualities they often display. It is not on the ground of any inferiority; but on that of the finer and more delicate organisation of body and brain, that I think even the " Ten Hours' Bill " an inadequate protection.

At the time that I first brought up this subject at the Social Science meeting at Bradford in 1859, I confined my observations to the surplus in the profession of the teacher. I took the statistics of the Governesses' Benevolent Institution in Harley Street, and urged as remedies for the terrible destitution endured by aged ladies, that parents of the middle-class should either train their daughters to some useful art, however humble, or consider it their primary duty to insure their lives if they could

not afford to lay by money for their female children. I showed that, in a country like England,
whose wealth is chiefly derived from commerce, the
fluctuations of trade fall with peculiar hardship upon
the defenceless sex. That not only do merchants
fail, but banks also break, and that a horrible
amount of real hunger and cold is undergone by
many who have been ladies born and bred; while a
larger proportion, though they may never know actual physical want, are forced into one overcrowded
and perhaps distasteful profession, in which they
spend their lives working for small salaries.

But I was far from contemplating the mass of
women becoming bread-winners to a greater extent than at present obtains. With the greatest
esteem for, and even gratitude to, many masters
for the pains which they take for the instruction
and *moralisation* of their workwomen, I do not
believe our English factory system to be natural,
and more especially the employment of married
women away from their homes. I know all that
may be said upon the other side ; I know that any
legislation on this topic would result in practical
cruelty; that even rules imposed by the master of

the factory would bear with harshness on the woman who may have a family to support, and a drunken or incapable husband. I believe that it is a point upon which we must allow free trade, or that we shall fall into worse evils than those from which we now suffer. Nevertheless, the fact remains clear to my mind, that we are passing through a stage of civilisation which is to be regretted, and that her house and not the factory is a woman's happy and healthful sphere.

It is not possible to treat a subject like this in a scientific way. Philosophers who argue upon the laws which govern the development of men are almost always destined to see their theories pass away or fade into comparative oblivion before the century which gave them birth is gone. Rousseau is seldom heard of now; Fourier exists only as the prophet of a school; even the Political Economists no longer reign over the intellectual world as they did thirty years ago, when the poor-law achieved the practical experiment of some of their principles. If, then, theories respecting masses of men are continually being broken to pieces, how much more impossible is it to argue from abstractions upon the nature of women; for a woman's life is certainly more individual, more centred in one house and one circle; and so it must be until the constitution of this world is changed. I can therefore only speak of women as I have seen and known them in different towns of this our country: in Birmingham, in Nottingham, in Edinburgh, in Dublin, in Leicester, in Hastings, in Glasgow. I speak of what I have seen of the lower classes, and of what I have heard from innumerable ladies, wives and daughters of squires, clergymen, doctors, lawyers, merchants. My opinions have been formed from these sources of information; and though I have found such ladies always willing and anxious in any plan for getting employment for their destitute sisters, I have always heard them lament when, from any circumstances, the family life of a district has suffered by the withdrawal of any large number of women from the home.

Of the home life I wish to speak without cant, and even for my present purpose without sentiment; I prefer to look at it simply in a broad religious point of view. A general notion of

SOCIAL ECONOMY. 221

Christianity lies at the bottom of the constitution
of every country of Europe, and the household
life in a Christian country has this very marked
characteristic, that it is the primary unit in social
organisation. The man alone, or the woman
alone, is not, strictly speaking, that primary unit.
With marriage and family life begins the great
social chain which ascends from the house to the
street, from the street to the parish, from the parish
to the town, from the town to the county, and
ends in the Government and in the Church.

The wife, in our civilisation, is the centre of
domestic and also of social life. She is the mistress of a social circle, and of a group of children
and of servants. When sensible men say that the
vast majority of women are destined to marriage,
what they mean—the idea which really lies at the
bottom of their minds is, that were it otherwise the
whole constitution of modern society would literally go to pieces. We should be like a house
built without mortar, ready to be blown down in
every high wind.

As I believe, therefore, firmly that the married
household is the first constituent element in na-

tional life, so I consequently believe that the immense majority of women are, and ought to be,
employed in the noble duties which go to make
up the Christian household; and while I fully
admit the principle of vocations to religious and
also to intellectual and practical life apart from
marriage, I think that people are quite right who
say that these will ever be, and ought ever to be,
in the minority.

In close connexion with all problems affecting
the welfare of the working-class is the science of
political economy. As it sanctions the producing
of national wealth, by means which it estimates on
arithmetical rather than on moral principles, it has
given a strong implied support to the employment
of women in great numbers in merely mechanical
pursuits. They are cheaper than men, therefore
use them; furthermore, they will probably always
be cheaper than men, because the man demands
wages equal to the support of a family, therefore
it will always be cheaper to use them. But as
moral beings, we are bound to consider and to re-
mark that political economy is simply a science,
and may be studied with or without reference to

practice; although it necessarily underlies the most ordinary life, sharing in this respect the nature of the most sublime physical sciences. Children and birds are familiarly said to go to bed with the sun, and are advised to get up in the same illustrious company; our dress changes with the variation of the temperature, and is modified by our distance from the tropics; meat freezes and milk turns sour by the various action of the same laws; water rising to its level fills our waterpipes; and smoke pours down our chimneys by the same principle which sweeps the rain-cloud through middle air. Science takes no cognizance of large or less, and exerts her powers with equal facility and equal exactitude for either. Just so we rent our houses, pay our poors' rate, fee our doctors, and add up our yearly bills, under the constraining force of some law of political economy, and like Moliere's hero, who had talked prose all his life without knowing it, we rarely pass a day without uttering sense or nonsense in regard to some of the topics investigated by Adam Smith or John Stuart Mill. When Maria cries her eyes out, because John is going to Australia, she is the unconscious victim of

" pressure of the population on the means of subsistence." When Sally leaves to better herself, and
the parlour is upset because the kitchen is in a
state of transition, it is the theory or the custom of
"wages" that is in question. When Cashmere
shawls are at a low figure, or cotton sheets cost
double, it arises from some change in the relations
of "demand and supply." The budget is only
Britannia's account book for household expenses,
helmets included, and John Bull has to look
sharply to his political economy on a large scale,
as to his arithmetic on a small one, under pain of
finding the shoe pinch severely soon or late.

This is, however, the most commonplace side
of the argument. Not by bread alone do men or
nations live ; nor for household uses only can any
woman live to whom God has granted means or
leisure. Political economy deals with questions of
charity, education, state relief of the poor, emigration, and occupation for all classes. None of these
things can a woman innocently ignore when they
are brought before her under their common names
of almsgiving, schooling, workhouses, &c. ; and in
none of them can she move without risk, unless

she follows some larger law than the mere pity of
the moment. For most women this larger law is
that of the gospel; and in a very small sphere, or
in a very simple state of society, its divine teaching
includes sufficient practical wisdom. But in our
extremely complex state of civilisation, where the
consequences of any movement act and react beyond our ken, some comprehension of the natural
social laws under which the world is governed is
necessary, even to the success of religious activity.
If we do not learn how to take advantage of these
laws, we shall certainly suffer by them, for they
have no more heart or conscience than the law of
gravity, by which the Hartley colliery was choked
up two years ago, and are as amenable to remon-
strance as the tides which swallowed up the Good-
win Sands. It has been asserted that "the sermon
on the mount forms the basis for the soundest system of political economy," but so far does this appear to me to be from the truth, that it is the discrepancy between the two dispensations which
constitutes one great difficulty of legislation, and
renders the conscientious discharge of private
charity a matter of much care. Those parts of

P

political economy which deserve the strict name of
science, are as invariable in their laws of action as
any department of human knowledge. As fire
burns, water drowns, and the electric bolt strikes
death into the frame of man, so do the operations
of commerce, while tending to secure the greatest
happiness of the greatest number, devour uncon-
cernedly any small obstacles in the way, human or
other. Indeed the laws of wealth are much more
fatal in their possible effect, for the element of sin
in human nature penetrates largely into the mere
scientific relations of trade; and whereas fire,
water, and electricity act with comparative independence of men, and only injure those who fall
directly in their way, and are rarely employed for
purposes of actual murder, the laws of political
economy are constantly being appropriated with
evil interest, or handled with such wicked careless-
ness that the greatest cruelties are perpetrated by
their aid. Thereupon arises one of the most difficult of all questions in modern society—How far to
interfere? in what way the principle of benevolence, having its root in the principle of Christianity, can be brought in well and wisely as a

counteractive of the evil or the selfish dealings of
men ?

Let none think this a mere question of long
words. It is being fought out every day, and
with an increasing tendency to apply the Christian
remedy. Thirty years ago, when first political
economy acquired the attitude and the dignity of
a science, people were so bewitched with its clearness, its firm granite basis of thought, the unerring
certainty of its law in action, that the best and
most benevolent thinkers placed the future of the
human race at its feet. But thirty years have done
much to undeceive us. It is true that the thought
is correct, the laws are sure, yet the people somehow get ground under the machinery. Assuredly
it is their own fault, or somebody else's fault ;
collectively we should get out of the way, and not
beat the table when we run against it ; but it 's a
hard matter ; hard to the stupid, the ignorant, the
weak ; and the foolish folk get a trick of dying
every day, not because the laws of political economy are disregarded, but because they take their
swing without cognisance of individual life, and are
even capable of being employed to its injury.

It is in the processes of production that the greatest complications arise, because they are now necessarily on a very large scale, each trade involving thousands upon thousands in its folds, and affording peculiar temptation to greediness and ambition of a lower kind. Also because the massing of human beings together is in itself a fearful and prolific source of evil, hard to counteract. A few words will explain how much pains may be required, on the one head of production, to harmonise the laws of economy with the laws of the gospel.

A great quantity of everything constitutes national wealth, and national wealth is the *summum bonum* of the economist; corn, wine, and oil, purple and fine linen ; blankets for everybody, and clean shirts without stint, good brick houses, and glass in the windows. Of course, to get all this, 1st, the producing machines must be as perfect as possible ; 2d, there must be no discouragement to the investment of capital. Let us take these two points separately.

Firstly, The producing machines must be as perfect as possible. We must not be content with old slow, cumbrous inventions, or stupid heads to manage them. If we get a better mechanism, or can hear of more intelligent workmen, we must by all means change for the better, and that without delay. Now this would be very well if the agents employed in production were all inanimate ; or if, being animate, they had no *other* use, no *other* faculty, than that of producing wealth. Let us break up our old iron, and burn our old wood ; let us send our old plough to the shed, and our old spinning wheel to Wardour Street, and set up bran new ones ; these things have but one use, but one aim ; if they cannot fulfil that, let them be sacrificed without remorse. But the human machine the brain, which we require to keep our iron wheels going suppose *that* is slow, cumbrous, and behind the times, what must we do ? Unfortunately, this brain is not self-existent, it is indissolubly connected with a stomach, and not unfrequently with a heart. Considered in the light of a producing brain merely, we certainly ought to show it no favour ; if it is deficient in concentrativeness, if it slopes back at an uncomfortable angle, if it is squeezed down flat over the eyes, or peaks up with unnatural sharpness, if its eyes have what George Elliot admirably terms a " bovine gaze," and its mouth chiefly opens to eat rather than to express the feast of reason and the flow of the soul, let us have none of it. If we trust to it for our corn, oil, and wine, purple and fine linen, blankets and shirts, we shall come off short, and somebody will have to go without.

But, unfortunately, this brain belongs to *A Man*, and the creature was so absurd as to get married, and four or five other young brains, flat, sloping, or peaked, are the result ; which again are linked to four or five hungry young stomachs, and hearts about which we don't know much, but which we are not quite easy in crushing if we come too near the operation. All these unproductive creatures whom we do see, are to be sent adrift in order that somebody whom we don't see may have blankets and shirts. This, too, is putting it in the simplest way, and one which does not include the whole question. If it were physical want against physical want, we might sacrifice the flat-brained creature, in spite of his unpleasant proximity ; but, unfortunately, there are spiritual problems in

volved, of which Christians must be dimly con-
scious. What if this ugly, tiresome creature be
called Lazarus? What if he be even the hidden
sign and the type of somewhat else? Are we then
to sacrifice him to the greatest good of the greatest
number viewed in relation to blankets and sheets?

This question is exactly what had to be answered
when stockings were first made by machinery, and
it is what has to be answered now, when high
farming and large farms are "improving" our
peasantry in many parts of this kingdom off the
face of the land. It is a difficulty which John
Stuart Mill has fairly contemplated, and it is one
which can only be met by great individual care
and thoughtfulness in the working out of trade
operations; in fact, by effort of conscience and of
religion. In his chapters upon the natural tendency of labour to flow like water where wages are
awaiting it, he more than admits, he shows the
great difficulty experienced by the labouring class
in moving from one part of the country to another,
in breaking up old habits and old associations, and
still more in changing work. Ditching may be
poorly paid, and bricklayers may be in request, but

how shall Mudges, already come to ripe middle age, learn to sit astride on a scaffold, and keep his lines by rule and plummet? How shall the weaver, with pale attenuated face and delicate fingers, turn to the forge, because the loom affords scanty profits? There is a period in human life when none, not even the most gifted, attain to new arts with ease; what, then, can be done with a hopeless Mudges? Assuredly, if these changes are attempted *en gros*, the most frightful misery must ensue, often has ensued; and nothing but forethought, patience, and absence of hasty greed on the part of the capitalist can avert it. If he seeks merely his rights according to the laws of political economy, God help the poor!

The case of the dressmakers involves a kindred argument. Not only does political economy require the machines to be of the best kind, it also requires that as much work should be got out of them as possible. Each additional hour is so much profit on the "sunk capital." If I have built a mill, and bought spinning-jennies, and got up my steam, I had better keep it going all night. If I have hired workrooms, fitted up my showrooms with marone velvet, laid in splendid material from Paris, and purchased twenty young women in fair and open market, it is undoubtedly my interest to work them to the utmost point consistent with keeping the life in them. If, indeed, I could get no more young women when these twenty were worked up, I should have to make a sharp calculation as to the resisting force of their constitutions, compared with their labour and supply of necessary nourishment. But as the conditions of the market are just now (and have been for some time past) in my favour, and I can get any number of girls so cheap, I need not trouble myself about working them up, provided I keep on the right side of a coroner's inquest. Even as regards niggers, some economists have thought it was cheapest to finish them off, and buy new ones. And you know I do not, strictly speaking, *buy*, I hire, which is so much in my favour, as on hiring I only bargain for so much disposable health and strength, and can cast aside the shell when the said health and strength is too much worn away. Sewing machines, too; that is a point to be considered; fewer girls will suffice me; and those who are turned off must be content to wait until the sewing factories are started; *then*, of course, they will get more employment.

In the meantime, the young dressmaker is in a condition extremely similar to that of Mudges. She does not know anything but her one trade, other things are extremely difficult to her; she was not very bright, and was apprenticed early, and though she and her sisters, being really surplus water, ought to flow away gracefully to Australia and New Zealand, where demand is active and supply small, there are difficulties in the way besides want of passage-money; there is an old mother who cannot be moved, and Mary Jane, who never went beyond Gravesend in her life, shrinks in mortal terror from the "unknown sea," and her wits, originally small, dwindle away to nothing at the notion, and, however lamentable the alternatives of her choice may be, she will probably choose one or other of them in preference to emigration.

Such are the difficulties which interpose between the natural adjustments of labour and wages, difficulties most painful to contemplate, because the

misery of an overstocked trade remains as an in-
dubitable fact which no sentiment of compassion
for the sufferers can remove. The fall of Humpty
Dumpty, in the nursery ballad, was not more irre-
trievable than is the fall of a manufacture or a
trade, when it can be no longer profitably carried
on; as well ask corn to grow on a bare rock, or
stones to sustain themselves in a bog, as demand
wages from a business losing to the employers.
This brings us to the second point laid down,
namely, the danger of interfering (by any kind of
legislation, for instance) with the motives which
induce people to save up capital.

Business cannot be started, nor farms bought,
without a sum of money in hand; and neither men
nor women will deny themselves the full enjoyment of their income, and lay it up for such
schemes, unless they expect to get a larger income
by and by. If one milliner were obliged to keep
on employing her girls, instead of changing them
for sewing machines, her profits would be less, and
her motives for choosing the millinery business
diminished. If *all* milliners were so restricted,
they would probably " put it on " to their custom-

ers, and everybody would pay dearer for their clothes. This was practically the state of things in the guilds of the middle ages, where the work-people were protected, first by apprenticeship, and then by the limited number of admissions to the trade. It would not be possible in a short space to express the reasons why such arrangements cannot now be carried on. The immense increase of population, and the whole genius of modern life, is against them, and we must allow people to use their money as they like, and be quite sure that if they are hindered, the only effect will be to starve that particular branch of industry.

Such is the rule universally admitted now. It has, however, exceptions, and these exceptions are so curious, and so illustrative of the moral laws which penetrate society, that they deserve particular attention, especially from women, who are the subjects of most of these anomalies. The first is the famous "Ten Hours' Bill." It is impossible to defend it on the ground of pure political economy; it is a restriction on the rights of capital, and makes it illegal for the workwoman to sell more than ten hours of her own time. Accordingly, when it was proposed, the manufacturers and the political economists opposed it as a measure suggestive of the dark ages, flying right in the face of the new science. Women, regarded by them in the light of working animals, ought, said they, to be the best judges of how long they could work, and what wages they needed to earn. It was tyranny to compel them to stop at a certain point. The struggle was very sharp, for the arguments had an enlightened sound, and these are days when enlightenment has set up a special cant of its own. One good and great man had the courage to fight this battle, upholding a moral truth in the face of a purely material science, and insisting year by year that the lower principle should be forced to a compromise. It is an intricate question whether or no Lord Shaftesbury's famous measure did or did not damp the investment of capital by checking the supply of labour. The development of the cotton trade has been so enormous of late years that any such check has been quite swallowed up in the general result. But no one now doubts that the bill was a right and good thing ; that it has saved a generation of women from disease and from a life of slavery. The moral sense of the country has rallied to it, and the sin against pure political economy is forgiven and forgotten. Another example is to be found in the enactments against the employment of women and children in mines. Children may perhaps come under a different category ; but if a woman wishes to earn her bread by drawing a truck on all-fours, under circumstances too which are best omitted in these pages, has she not every right, as a free-born Briton, to comport herself as a beast ? No, said Lord Shaftesbury ; no, said public opinion ; no, at last, said Parliament, in flagrant violation of pure political economy.

The overwork of dressmakers is fairly to be looked upon in a similar light. Abstractly the mistress and her " hands" are supposed to be on equal terms ; if the one can refuse to pay, the other can refuse to work, and the see-saw of their interests ought strictly speaking to produce a fair level of wages for the employed. But while the possession of capital always puts its owner in a position of great superiority, it does so more particularly in the case of women. The girls cannot " strike" as

men can ; they are unused to band together, they
have nothing to turn to as a means of livelihood,
and they are far more fragile in health and nerves.
It is matter of every-day experience that they can
be oppressed heavily by the mere custom of the
trade, and there is a point at which the moral
sense of society revolts, and interferes to protect.
If a bill be brought into Parliament to limit the
hours during which milliners' workshops can be
left open, it will meet with a certain amount of
opposition from political economists, on grounds
which are logically irrefragable, but it will probably
be carried in spite of them, because the instincts of
humanity refuse to sanction the immediate sacrifice
of human life to the slow working out of an economical law.

Such are a few of the problems to be met with
even in this science which seem so plain and definite. It is only by considering men and women
as mere wealth-producing animals that we steer
clear of hindrance. It is certain that by any in-
fraction of its laws less wealth will be created ;
there is no escaping *that* conclusion. But while
wine, purple and fine linen are not actual neces-

saries for the human race, and should be instantly sacrificed for higher considerations, even blankets and sheets and cotton shirts for the million may be dearly purchased, if, owing to the complex conditions of our civilised state, the price of their unrestricted production is the death of " one of these little ones."

Ballantyne, Roberts, & Company, Printers, Edinburgh.

For EU product safety concerns, contact us at Calle de José Abascal, 56–1°, 28003 Madrid, Spain or eugpsr@cambridge.org.

www.ingramcontent.com/pod-product-compliance
Ingram Content Group UK Ltd.
Pitfield, Milton Keynes, MK11 3LW, UK
UKHW010340140625
459647UK00010B/720